Birds

OF WESTERN NORTH AMERICA

Birds

OF

Western North America

NONPASSERINES

PAINTINGS BY

KENNETH L. CARLSON

TEXT BY

LAURENCE C. BINFORD

MACMILLAN PUBLISHING CO., INC.

NEW YORK

COLLIER MACMILLAN PUBLISHERS

LONDON

LIBRARY OF CONGRESS CATALOGING IN PUBLICATION DATA

Binford, Laurence Charles, 1935–
  Birds of Western North America.

  1. Birds—The West.   2. Birds—North America.
I. Carlson, Kenneth L., illus. II. Title.
QL683.W4B53   598.2'978   74-7350
ISBN 0-02-510900-6

Macmillan Publishing Co., Inc.
866 Third Avenue, New York, N. Y. 10022
Collier-Macmillan Canada Ltd.

First Printing 1974

Printed in the United States of America

Contents

 Preface

The fifty species treated in this volume are confined to the nonpasserine families and were selected for their physical attractiveness, biological interest, and taxonomic variety from those birds that, in the North American portions of their ranges, are most common in the West. The portraits are executed in gouache, the medium with which the artist feels he can best attain reality in the varied textures of the birds and background materials.

The text is designed not only to inform, but also to entertain the reader whose appetite has been whetted and whose curiosity has been aroused by the paintings. To this end, the author has employed a free essay style rather than a categorized text of dry predigested facts and has stressed the more unusual and interesting aspects of avian biology. Frequently, a species is used to illustrate a scientific principle or to point out gaps in our knowledge. For each species, information is presented on size, range, habitat, diet, nest, eggs, and familial relationships. In many cases, vocalizations and behavior are also covered. Details of field identification and seasonal plumage variation, readily available in field guides, usually are not included. The nomenclature and sequence follow the *Check-list of North American Birds* (fifth edition, American Ornithologists' Union, 1957) and its thirty-second supplement (*Auk* 90:411–419).

We wish to extend our sincere appreciation to the following personnel of the California Academy of Sciences, who afforded the use of their collections and gave freely of their time and knowledge: Dr. Paul H. Arnaud, Jr., Dr. Dennis E. Breedlove, Lillian J. Dempster, Dr. Warren C. Freihofer, Frederick Funk, John T. Hjelle, Johan Kooy, Hugh B. Leech, Dr. Elizabeth McClintock, Dr. Robert T. Orr, and Diana R. Young. Charlotte Dorsey ably typed the manuscript, and Karen Hakanson and Jacqueline Schonewald aided in reading proof.

Painting the birds in such detail would have been impossible without the bird collections of the California Academy of Sciences and the Museum of Vertebrate Zoology, University of California, Berkeley, the latter made available by Dr. Ned K. Johnson. The resources of the J. D. Randall Junior Museum and the San Francisco Zoological Gardens provided the artist with the opportunity to observe many of the species alive and at close range; access to the latter was kindly afforded by Ronald T. Reuther and Paul Maxwell.

We are especially indebted to Ted and John Kipping of the Strybing Arboretum and Botanical Gardens, who never forgot to watch for appropriate plants while on field trips and went to great lengths in collecting and even growing the required specimens. A gold star is awarded to Mary Lea Carlson, who served as the artist's secretary, collector, and critic and relieved him of many duties while he was totally engrossed in painting.

Finally, we would like to thank the following for their special contributions: Gary Bogue, Ron Brixen, Elaine Eilers, Tom Eilers, Barbara Ingle, Rex Reynolds, Kerry Schmidt, Mary Rose Spivey, and Dr. Robert W. Storer.

Laurence C. Binford
Kenneth Carlson

Introduction

THROUGH the combined media of art and literature, we wish to instill in the reader an increased appreciation and awareness of the beauty and fascination inherent in the world of birds. No one, however, can fully appreciate birds until he has first observed them in their natural state and then investigated their biology. Accordingly, this introduction is designed to inspire the uninitiated to embrace birding as a hobby and to encourage the experienced amateur to delve into the scientific aspects of ornithology, even to the extent of initiating research leading to the publication of new information.

BIRDING AS A HOBBY

WHAT. The term *bird-watching*, broadly defined, means simply looking at birds. In its more specific sense, however—now called *birding*—it is the sport of purposely seeking out and identifying avian species. The extent to which a person embraces the hobby is a matter of personal preference. Many find that their commitment evolves from mere feeder-watching to world travel. Some people never leave their yards, others go afield only once or twice a year, and the more ambitious set forth every weekend. Some prefer to work local areas, whereas others travel thousands of miles per year and even take birding vacations. One couple put 50,000 birding miles on their car in a single year in California alone. After I moved to San Francisco, one of my first trips was a 1,500-mile, two-day whirlwind tour of southern California.

Those who aspire to become experts should not take up the sport lightly, for there is much to be learned. There are over 800 species in North America north of México. In many of these, plumage varies according to geography, sex, age, season, wear, color phase, and individual peculiarities. In some hawks, notably the red-tailed (*Buteo jamaicensis*), variation is almost infinite. As a result, a birder must learn not 800, but several thousand plumages. In addition, the expert must know vocalizations (most species have several), range, habitat, general behavior, flying and perching silhouettes and mannerisms, and taxonomic relationships. Extend these many details to the 8,700 species of birds in the world, and the challenge in birding becomes readily apparent. Although the birder can never hope to master all aspects of the hobby, neither will he become bored.

WHO. Anyone can play the game, from tot to great-grandmother, backpacker to shut-in. Many people are bird watchers in the broad sense of the word without realizing it. Thousands of citizens maintain feeding stations or nest boxes in their yards, and sportsmen often become skilled in identifying their quarry. Have you ever admired a swirling flock of gulls; stirred to a wedge of honking geese high overhead; or questioned the identity of a bird that flitted through your yard, eyed your fishing line, or narrowly escaped your bouncing golf ball? If you have, you are already a bird watcher. If you enjoyed it, spend a few dollars for a good field guide, dig out that old pair of binoculars, and become a birder. It may change your life.

WHY. To explain the attraction of birding is difficult, for it is a personal matter. Certainly the challenge is important. Many people simply enjoy watching the varied shapes, colors, and behavior of birds. Others like the physical exercise or the mental relaxation from daily employment. For still others, birding provides a convenient excuse to get out-of-doors or to travel. Virtually every birder enjoys the camaraderie of the sport. One of the strongest of fraternities, birding attracts people from all over the world and from all walks of life. I firmly believe that I could travel the circumference of the United States and spend every night in the home of a fellow birder.

Perhaps the primary impetus, however, may be summed up in one word: listing. Man has within himself the innate desire to collect things, be they stamps, bottle caps, or bird eggs. For the modern birder, this drive has been transferred to amassing lists of bird records. Nearly every birder maintains a "life list"—a compilation of all the species he has recorded in the wild during his lifetime. Most "listers" keep a North American list; a total of 600 species entitles the observer to membership in the famous 600 Club. Lists may be compiled for country, state or province, county, yard, or window. Time provides another basis for listing; hence, the daily, monthly, or yearly lists. These may be combined with regional lists to form the annual state list, daily county list, and the like. The possibilities are endless.

The acme of bird listing is the Big Day. In this endeavor, a single party attempts to see as many species as possible within a single calendar day. Each participant (four or five is ideal) must remain at all times within conversational speaking distance of his companions. Plans are laid well in advance. The itinerary is mapped and timed, and the difficult species are located by precensusing. Because the starting point may be hundreds of miles from home, a party may have to remain alert for well over the twenty-four hours allotted for the count. It is a good idea to take a Big Day on a Saturday, leaving Sunday for recuperation! At midnight the party is stationed at a known owling locality. To save time, which is the most critical factor, an owl may be called up early so that it may be heard and checked off at the stroke of twelve. Then the race is on, with the most competent (and fastest) driver at the helm. The record for all Big Days in North America (north of México) is 229, obtained by a party of four in southern Texas. Because few localities can hope to compete with this incredible total, most Big Days are run on a local basis in an attempt to break the previous high for the same area.

Whether personal or competitive, such lists are compiled simply for fun. They can, however, assume some degree of scientific value if carefully embellished with dates, localities, and numbers of individual birds. Listing automatically leads to the search for regional rarities, the discovery of which provides the driving force for many birders. If, after compiling a list, a person is suddenly seized with the compulsion to add to it or to break the personal high that it established, he is hooked; he has become a lister.

How. *Equipment.* The first step in becoming a birder is to select the proper equipment. Of the several field guides available for western North America, by far the best, in my opinion, is *A Field Guide to Western Birds* by Roger Tory Peterson (second edition. Boston: Houghton Mifflin Co., 1961). The plates stress patterns rather than individual feathers; hence the beginner sees in his guide what he observes at a distance in the field and is not confused by fine details that are useless in identification. Peterson stresses *field marks*, those specific characteristics of a bird that individually or collectively allow identification. Perhaps the most useful portion of the book, however, is its text section on similar species, which allows the elimination of all birds with which the unknown can be confused.

The most important item of birding equipment is a pair of binoculars. Critical points to consider are brand, price, weight, bulk, magnification, and diameter of the objective lenses. I prefer to purchase the best that I can afford. Usually, quality can be judged by price. Bausch and Lomb, Bushnell, and Zeiss are excellent brands. In high-quality binoculars, the optics provide sharper visibility and minimal eye strain, and the solid construction better withstands rough usage. To judge lens quality, observe an object and compare the center of the field of view with the extreme edge, checking for a color fringing effect and physical distortion; the best binoculars exhibit only slight differences.

Lightweight, rather small binoculars are preferable, as they produce less strain on neck and arms and can be held and focused more easily. However, a compromise must be effected between these factors, the power, and the objective lens diameter. Each pair of binoculars has two numbers printed on it; for example, 7 × 35. The first number means that the image appears seven times closer. Because the natural vibrations of hands are magnified by the power (seven times in this example), the average person should not consider glasses over seven or eight power. Only people with very steady hands can comfortably hold glasses as high as ten power. Powers under seven are, in my opinion, too weak.

The second number on the binoculars is the diameter, in millimeters, of each of the objective (front) lenses. The wider the lens, the more light it will collect. By dividing the lens diameter by the power and squaring the result, one obtains the relative brightness of the binoculars; for example, $(50 \div 7)^2 = 50.5$. The higher this value, the brighter the image will appear, and the more detail the eye will be able to see. Although glasses with a relative brightness as low as 25 are adequate, I recommend those with a value over 40. The width of the field of view, which depends on the optical system and power, should be as great as possible; usually, it is listed in the accompanying brochure. The ideal pair of binoculars does not exist; final selection must be based on personal preference tempered with a working knowledge of the points discussed above.

Listing techniques are myriad and depend on personal taste and the type and amount of data to be recorded. Many people use a lined notebook, writing out the names of every bird seen. The American Birding Association, which handles records from hundreds of people all over the continent, has gone so far as to computerize the data. This organization also advertises a variety of forms for listing. For the beginner I recommend starting with a field card system. Field cards, obtainable from local bird societies, are printed, pocket-sized lists of all the birds occurring in a given region. Most cards have spaces for checking off each species and for recording at least the date, locality, and observers. Although designed for daily use, these cards are convenient for making almost any kind of list. In the final analysis, each person must develop his own system; and for the inveterate lister, many happy hours may be consumed in this pursuit.

One field guide, a good pair of binoculars, and listing materials are the only essential equipment. Eventually, however, the birder will desire supplementary aids. The most complete set of phonograph records of bird voices is *A Field Guide to Western Bird Songs* (Boston: Houghton Mifflin Co.), which is arranged to accompany the Peterson field guide. In aquatic habitats a good telescope is almost a necessity. I would recommend the BALscope, Sr., with a single 20× or 30× eyepiece. Turret mounts are useful, but difficult to aim. Zoom scopes are quite popular, but to my mind they lose so much in brightness and definition at the higher powers that the extra expense outweighs the advantages. Of utmost importance is the tripod. It must be small and light enough to be carried easily, but steady enough to withstand vibrations from the earth and winds. It must have retractable legs and a single handle control for both vertical and lateral movements. Elevators and other accessories produce undesirable vibrations.

The birder will also feel the need of additional literature. Of the thousands of books that have been published, I would single out the following as "musts" for any library: *A Guide to Bird Watching* by Joseph J. Hickey (New York: Oxford University Press, 1943), *Ornithology in Laboratory and Field* by Olin Sewall Pettingill, Jr. (fourth edition. Minneapolis: Burgess Publishing Company, 1970), the three-volume set of Audubon bird guides by Richard H. Pough (Garden City, N. Y.: Doubleday and Company, Inc., 1949, 1951, and 1957), *A New Dictionary of Birds* by A. Landsborough Thomson (New York: McGraw-Hill Book Company, 1964), *The Life of Birds* by Joel Carl Welty (New York: Alfred A. Knopf, 1963), and the most recent and complete distributional state book. Many journals also are available. For the hobbyist, I suggest *American Birds* (950 Third Avenue, New York, N. Y. 10022), *Birding* (American Birding Association, Box 4335, Austin, Texas), and a state or local periodical.

The proper selection of wearing apparel will avoid many unhappy hours. So many times I have seen a birder (often myself) shivering uncomfortably because of a sudden change of weather. Clothes can always be removed for cooling, but cannot be added if left at home. Those who bird from cars, as most of us do, have few space limitations and can go prepared for anything. Always follow this cardinal rule: take more clothes (and foot gear) than you think you will need; if in doubt, take it.

Technique. A few hints will enable the beginner to develop the proper field technique more quickly. He should study the field guide diligently, committing to memory the following information: the format of the text; the external topography of a "typical" bird; the vernacular names and sequence of families; the total lengths of the common crow (*Corvus brachyrhynchos*), American robin (*Turdus migratorius*), and house sparrow (*Passer domesticus*) or house finch (*Carpodacus mexicanus*); and the common names and field marks on the plates.

Since in the field an unknown bird may disappear at any moment, the observer should not take time to refer to the guide until he has systematically scrutinized the bird from head to foot, noting all characteristics of pattern, color, size, and shape. The overall size and shape of the bird, together with the configurations of the bill and feet, often reveal family relationships. The presence or absence of wing bars, superciliary line, eye-ring, whisker marks, and tail spots are frequently important. Voice, actions, and flight shape may be diagnostic. The spotted sandpiper (*Actitis macularia*), for example, "teeters" as it walks; the osprey (*Pandion haliaetus*) flies with its wings bowed downward; alcids open their wings prior to submergence; many sparrows hop, whereas pipits walk. Once satisfied that he has seen everything, the observer should thumb from plate to plate until he discovers a likely candidate, compare each of its field marks directly with the bird in question, and finally, for confirmation, read the text section on similar species. Identification snowballs; with each identification, the next becomes easier.

Of all the attributes that a birder can develop, the most important is accuracy. Speed of identification is desirable, but accuracy is imperative. Even for experts, many factors may preclude identification: extreme distance; intervening vegetation; poor visibility owing to lighting, fog, or precipitation; tearing eyes resulting from strong winds; brevity of observation time; and simple inexperience. Nothing is more exasperating than to obtain a good view of a bird and then be unable to find it in the book because of failure to note the one critical field mark. The careful observer never lets himself be talked into an identification, but strives for complete intellectual honesty. This may sound easy, but it is not, for the temptation to add another species to the list is very strong. Once, on the waterfront of Chicago, I discovered a winter-plumaged adult little gull (*Larus minutus*) perched on a nearby piling. Having made a

previous study of this species, I was able to point out to my companion, Charles T. Clark, the several obscure field marks that made the identification certain. Although Charlie carefully noted each criterion and was convinced that I was correct, he never counted the bird on his own lists because he himself could not vouch for its identity. This is the degree of caution for which one should strive.

Time and patience are required to master bird voices, but a knowledge of at least a few songs is a necessity, because some species, notably in the flycatcher genus *Empidonax*, are virtually inseparable by other criteria. Not only is there much to remember, but the beginner will soon find that he must train himself even to *hear* the varied frequencies and qualities of bird vocalizations. As a youngster, I spent ten minutes straining to hear a northern parula (*Parula americana*) that my companions assured me was singing virtually overhead. Because my ear was not tuned in to the particular pitch and buzzy quality of the song, I was unable to hear it until I actually watched the bird open its mouth. Subsequently, I had no difficulty. Phonograph recordings are very helpful, but in the final analysis there is no substitute for field experience. The technique is easy: simply trace down any unknown voice to its originator. Having an expert at hand will save a great deal of time and effort.

When in the field, the observer should cultivate the ability to walk quietly and without watching his feet, allowing his eyes to roam freely and continuously. Exposed perches should be scrutinized for bird silhouettes, the sky searched for dark specks, and the vegetation watched for bright colors and for movement unassociated with windblown branches. In open habitats, such as mud flats, large bodies of water, or prairies, binoculars or a scope may be used for scanning. However, the general rule in birding, especially in closed habitats, is to find birds with the naked eye and use optical equipment only to obtain the closer view needed for identification.

Many a secretive bird may be induced from dense vegetation by a high-pitched, mouselike noise, called "squeaking," that apparently resembles a wounded bird or mammal and is especially attractive to raptors and shorebirds. It may be produced by kissing the back of the hand or by using the lips only. The latter method frees the hands to hold binoculars. Another sound, called "shushing," may have even better results. It is accomplished by producing the sound *pish* with lips, mouth, and breath only, without vocal cords. When employing these techniques, the birder should conceal himself in vegetation, remain motionless, and broadcast loudly to attract distant birds. In one fifteen-minute bout of shushing in Washington State, I attracted twenty-eight species to within ten feet of me. Some territorial birds are easily lured into view by imitation of their calls. Although whistled or voiced imitations often are adequate, tape recordings are better. This technique is especially advantageous with nocturnal species, such as owls; but diurnal forms also respond, sometimes to the extent of attacking the machine. Although one will feel ridiculous as he produces peculiar sounds to the stares and giggles of passersby, he should persevere—the rewards will outweigh the embarrassment.

WHERE. One of the advantages of the birding hobby is that it may be pursued virtually anywhere in the world. Even the arctic ice fields, Arabian deserts, and vast oceans harbor a few species at some times of the year. The best and fastest method of learning local birding areas is to join organized field trips, either private or public. Nearly every bird club sponsors field trips, some publish bird-finding information, and a few offer recorded phone messages detailing the whereabouts of the latest unusual sightings.

If none of these aids is available, the initiate must kindle his exploratory instincts and go it alone. He must be mobile in thought and action, investigating habitats of all types and localities both near and far. Desert oases, islands, and coastal land projections often are profitable, for they act as traps to concentrate migrants. Although a long hike may be necessary to obtain a specific bird and is valuable in allowing intimacy with a few, rarely will it produce variety. Most enthusiasts therefore bird by vehicle.

Vacations may be planned to take in more distant regions of North America, each of which offers species difficult or impossible to find elsewhere. México is well within the range and means of the average birder and will provide hundreds of species not found farther north. The possibilities are endless. For bird-finding information on a continental scale, birders rely on word of mouth and regional books. *A Guide to Bird Finding West of the Missis-sippi* by Olin Sewall Pettingill, Jr. (New York: Oxford University Press, 1953), although somewhat out of date, is still helpful. The American Birding Association publishes more up-to-date hints in its journal, *Birding*.

WHEN. Birding can and should be pursued throughout the year, regardless of weather, for great seasonal changes in the avifauna are wrought by biannual migrations. Land birds, especially in hot regions, are most active in the mornings and late afternoons. I like to spend the evening hours watching birds go to roost in a marsh. Night birding for owls and goatsuckers should not be neglected. When birding on the Pacific coast, observers should take into account the effects of tides, for what may be a shorebird-strewn mud flat one hour may be a birdless expanse of blue the next. Lighting also plays a role. Thus trips to the Pacific ocean should be planned for morning, before reflections cast by the western sun make scanning impossible.

ORNITHOLOGY AND THE AMATEUR

In North America during the latter part of the nineteenth century, active field men consisted largely of vocational ornithologists, together with private and professional collectors. Although some of these pioneers carried binoculars and doubtless attained some degree of skill in field identification, most of their work was accomplished over the barrel of a shotgun, for they were concerned with amassing collections to be used in describing new forms and delineating ranges. Time and interest permitted only a cursory approach to the studies of breeding biology and behavior. The true hobbyist, who simply watched birds for recreation, was a rare and little-known breed, perhaps to be tolerated but never taken seriously; for avian science did not accept unusual distributional records unless based on specimens.

In the year 1899, the National Audubon Society originated the journal *Bird-Lore* (now *Audubon*), which a year later began publishing seasonal observations and annual Christmas bird censuses, both based largely on sight records. Later these types of reports were to be combined and expanded in the separate journal *Audubon Field Notes*, now called

American Birds. Perhaps more than any other single factor, *Bird-Lore* was responsible for creating interest in birding and in lending at least an aura of credibility to the sight record. By the 1930s true experts were beginning to emerge, among them Ludlow Griscom, who led the way in demonstrating to the scientific community that birds could be identified accurately in the field without collecting. In 1934, Roger Tory Peterson published the first of many editions of his famous book, *A Field Guide to the Birds* (mentioned earlier), which revolutionized the sport. Armed with modern optical equipment and an excellent guide, competent amateurs increased in number and gradually spread westward during the 1940s and 1950s. Science, however, still was not ready to accept fully the validity of sight records. As late as 1957, in its *Check-list of North American Birds* (fifth edition), the conservative American Ornithologists' Union indicated its opinion by ignoring the vast quantities of distributional sight data in *Audubon Field Notes.*

About that same time, however, the attitudes of even the old guard began to mellow as the younger generations of students proved their observational prowess by occasionally collecting rarities. Although these "upstarts" were schooled in the importance of collecting, they also realized the value and validity of sight records and soon were producing scholarly distributional works utilizing both types of data. Then in the 1960s came the ecology boom. Public opinion shifted, and birding was no longer considered solely the realm of the knicker-clad elderly. Logistical difficulties and moral objections made collecting difficult. Thousands of young people turned to the sport and, aided by experienced observers, quickly attained a degree of skill previously possessed by only a few gifted individuals. Finally, various organizations initiated procedures for validating documented sightings, and distributional papers based on observations alone began to appear in the major ornithological journals. This is where North American ornithology stands today. Although there must always remain a need for limited collecting, especially in the poorly explored regions of the continent, the sight record has come into its own.

As a consequence of this evolution, the amateur, especially the expert, now more than ever has an accepted place in the scientific world. I have always felt that the countless hours that the expert expends chasing birds from one corner of the world to another, although personally gratifying, are nevertheless somehow wasted. This is particularly true of the person whose urge is simply to accumulate bare lists, full of check marks but little information. How valuable these observations could be if recorded carefully and in detail.

The recording system need not be elaborate or overly time-consuming, but must be absolutely accurate. An incorrect record is far worse than no record at all, for somehow (perhaps years after the person's death) it may be published and the error perpetuated down through the ages. Minimal information on each day's trip should include the date, weather, names of companions, inclusive hours of observation, exact itinerary, and, most importantly, the number of individuals of each species seen at each locality. All rarities must be copiously and precisely documented; notes should take into account an exact description (shape, dimensions, plumage, soft parts, vocalizations, actions), conditions of observation (lighting, optical equipment, distance, length of time), habitat, and names of other observers. In addition, rarities should be reported immediately to the nearest birders so that they can confirm the sighting on the same day. Whereas distributional data are likely to be of major concern to the average birder, information on nesting, behavior, habitat preference, and anything else that comes to mind should also be documented. Writing notes while in the field is preferable, for by the time the observer returns home he will have forgotten many details or be too tired to record them.

The field card system previously recommended for listers is adaptable to the type of distributional record-keeping now under discussion, provided the cards have ample space. If no spacious card is available, the observer may wish to make his own. By using initials as abbreviations for localities (carefully noting the meaning of each on the card), one can record localities and numbers of individuals in the space provided after each species; for example, surf scoter, AB (126) I (3). Elsewhere on the card are the notations that AB=Abbott's Lagoon, Pt. Reyes, Marin Co., California and that I=Inverness, Marin Co., California. Additional notes may be written on blank cards or sheets of notebook paper and stapled to the checklist, with appropriate correlation by means of numbered asterisks. One small box will house hundreds of checklists. Some people record all data in blank notebooks. In my opinion, however, handwriting the name of a bird every time it is seen during a long day becomes tedious and requires too much observational time; also, the data are not easily retrievable. Distributional data may merit separate publication. In most cases, however, they should be submitted to *American Birds*, where they can be correlated with other observations to produce a meaningful trend.

I would like to encourage the highly experienced and competent birder to go a step farther and extend his interests to the more technical aspects of field ornithology. Two options are open: to assist an established program or to undertake totally independent research. If, for instance, an observer enjoys finding nests, he may attach himself to the national nest card program of the Cornell Laboratory of Ornithology (Ithaca, New York). Many birders already participate in the annual Christmas Bird Counts organized by the National Audubon Society in collaboration with the U. S. Fish and Wildlife Service (write to the editor of *American Birds*, 950 Third Avenue, New York, N. Y. 10022). These same organizations also coordinate and publish the results of Winter Bird-Population Studies and Breeding-Bird Censuses, both of which are fascinating and badly need additional workers. The Migratory Bird Populations Station (Laurel, Maryland 20810) directs the Breeding Bird Survey, a census designed to count birds along a set 25-mile stretch of road. Many avian programs conducted by biological stations, museums, schools, and bird observatories utilize volunteer help. Some well-qualified birders turn to birdbanding when their taste for the chase begins to wane.

Contrary to popular opinion, extensive biological training is not an absolute prerequisite for independent research. For many types of studies, one needs only time, great curiosity and patience, complete objectivity, and a passion for detail and accuracy. Most birders who merit the title of expert have these qualifications and can contribute much to our knowledge of birds. Dr. L. W. Walkinshaw, for example, a dentist by profession and birder by avocation, has become a world authority on cranes.

A birder may wish to use his expertise in field identification to undertake a comprehensive distributional study of an area or species. The number of other topics to be explored is legion. Here I must limit the discussion to one example: breeding biology. Published data on breeding biology often are abundant for those western species that range commonly into eastern North America or Europe, but seem to be extremely scanty for those that are restricted to the West. Prime examples are the surfbird (*Aphriza virgata*) and black turnstone (*Arenaria melanocephala*; see species account), but none of the fifty species treated herein has been studied thoroughly, and few even adequately. Perhaps the primary reason for this is that western ornithology is still young. Professional ornithologists and particularly scientifically inclined amateurs are still relatively scarce; many of the former are engaged in laboratory studies, and most of the latter have a strong bent for distribution.

The first step in conducting a study of breeding biology is to pick a species, preferably one that is endemic to western North America and builds an accessible nest. The study area should be near home and be free of human disturbance. The second step is to construct an outline for the type of study planned. I would suggest using the information given by Pettingill (1970, *op. cit.*) and by any comprehensive study of a related species to expand the outline presented by Hickey (*op. cit.*). Additional topics may come to mind later. The recent literature should be perused to see how modern life history studies have been conducted. The third step is to make a thorough search of the literature to determine the current state of our knowledge. I would suggest setting up two separate files of 3 × 5 cards, one for references (by author) and the other for information (by subject); the latter is used to quote (noting page numbers) every scrap of data uncovered in the literature and is cross-referenced to the author cards. Initial sources of information and references should include *Biological Abstracts, Zoological Record, Life Histories of North American Birds* (A. C. Bent, *et al.*, Bulletin U. S. National Museum, 1919–1968), and *Handbook of North American Birds* (Ralph S. Palmer, editor. Vol. 1. New Haven, Conn.: Yale University Press, 1962).

When these three steps have been accomplished, the real fun begins, for the investigator is now ready to observe his quarry, recording everything. The only essential pieces of equipment are binoculars, notebook, pen, and watch. A rough blind and a camera may be required, and a simple tape recorder is very handy for note-taking. Many schools and museums are willing to lend more sophisticated equipment, should it be desired, and some even offer access to computers. They will also identify plant specimens, food samples, and nest materials. Banding of the adults and young is advisable, even necessary if the sexes are similar. Although banding licenses can be obtained, it is far easier to seek the help of an established bander.

Data are worthless unless published. Because modern scientific writing has a unique style, the investigator may do well, when the time comes, to seek the advice of a professional. Editors are always helpful if the data warrant publication, but they cannot be expected to rewrite papers completely. Short articles may be submitted to *The Auk*, *The Condor*, *The Wilson Bulletin*, *Western Birds*, or any local journal that prints life history studies. Lengthy papers may be published in institutional or organizational series.

In this necessarily brief discussion, I have tried to demonstrate that observational field studies, especially those concerning breeding biology, are badly needed and that many expert amateur birders are qualified to conduct them. If only one reader accepts the challenge, I will have accomplished my mission.

Birds

OF WESTERN NORTH AMERICA

PLATE I

Arctic Loon

GAVIA ARCTICA

The frosted boreal sun sank to its subzenith in fruitless search of the horizon. Newly divested of its icy coat, the steel-gray lake shivered in the eerie half-light; and the dense primeval forest, responding to the stillness, settled its needled boughs into the lurking shadows. Suddenly, a bloodcurdling scream shattered the calm, and in the distance came, as if in commiseration, a long mournful wail. The arctic loons had returned.

This species is nearly circumpolar in its distribution, and its "loony" cries may be heard throughout the summer in both the arctic and boreal regions. In North America it breeds throughout much of Alaska east to the Melville Peninsula and Baffin Island and south to the northern portions of Saskatchewan, Manitoba, and Ontario. Each fall our American population shifts toward the west and southwest to winter along the Pacific coast from southeastern Alaska to the Gulf coast of Sonora and the tip of Baja California. On the northward journey in April and early May, thousands stream past the shores of California. Although largely restricted to salt water in the winter, during the summer this bird inhabits freshwater lakes and ponds in open or wooded, flat or mountainous terrain.

The arctic loon, or black-throated diver, as it is called in Europe, is a superior aquanaut. An average dive lasts about fifty seconds, but under duress a bird can remain submerged for more than three minutes. Anatomically, members of the loon family (Gaviidae) are strongly adapted for their aquatic life. The body is long, superbly streamlined, and clothed (except for the velvety head and neck) in a dense compact plumage. To provide maximum propulsion, the three front toes are very long and fully webbed. The tarsi are laterally compressed, so that when brought forward they cut through the water with as little friction as a knife blade. Because the tibiae are bound to the body and the legs are positioned so far to the rear—conditions producing great leverage in water—land progression may be accomplished only by wriggling along on the belly. So strong is their commitment to water that loons cannot become airborne from land, but must patter across water to attain the required speed.

In its marine winter quarters, the arctic loon leads a solitary existence or associates with only a few of its kind. Only during migration or when attracted to a common food source may it be found in larger numbers. It feeds on crustaceans, mollusks, insects, small fish, and aquatic plants.

The nest may be a large, rather flat mound built up of rotted vegetation in the shallow water of a slough or, more commonly, a sparsely lined depression on an island or at the periphery of a lake or large pond. The ground color of the two (rarely one or three) eggs is some shade of dark brown and is overlaid with spots and blotches of gray, lavender, and blackish brown.

Loon chicks have two sets of nestling down, produced from the same feather follicles. The first set, present at hatching, is pushed out by, and remains attached to, the tips of the second. In winter, adult arctics lose their striking pattern and assume a drab plumage similar to that of the immatures—dark gray above and white below.

PLATE 2

Eared Grebe

PODICEPS NIGRICOLLIS

During the summer the tiny eared grebe inhabits shallow lakes and ponds in portions of southwestern Canada and throughout the western United States, exclusive of the extreme Southwest and Northwest. It winters from the southern edge of its breeding range to Guatemala. Some half million birds are said to winter on the Salton Sea in California, and at the peak of spring migration in May, up to 20,000 congregate at Malheur National Wildlife Refuge in Oregon. This species is also widespread in Eurasia, where it is usually called the black-necked grebe.

In our West, the bird's mellow *poo-eep, poo-eep* or harsh *hicko-rick-up, hicko-rick-up, hicko-rick-up* may be heard issuing from the patches of emergent aquatic vegetation near which it nests. The nests are constructed of reeds and algae on top of floating debris in relatively open situations and are located in such dense colonies that they sometimes touch each other. In one instance a colony consisted of over twenty-five nests in an area measuring only ten by twenty feet. One pond in Alberta supported an estimated 2,000 pairs. The three hours of work necessary to build a nest is spread over several days. The three or four (occasionally one to six) eggs are an extremely pale greenish white or buffy white when first laid but soon become stained with darker buff or brown.

The toes of members of the grebe family (Podicipedidae), rather than being fully webbed as might be expected in an aquatic species, are broadly lobed, an adaptation that allows rapid underwater propulsion and at the same time convenient maneuverability among weeds and in soft-bottomed shallows, where full webs might produce an unwelcome sticking suction. The generic name, *Podiceps*, is from Latin and means "rump-footed," an allusion to the posterior positioning of the legs.

The bill of the eared grebe is wider than high and is slightly upturned, modifications perhaps of value in bottom feeding. Rather generalized in its food habits, this species takes frogs (including tadpoles), small fish, crustaceans, mollusks, leech eggs, a variety of insects and their larvae, and other invertebrates.

Grebes feed by diving, sometimes leaping clear of the surface as if to gain momentum. When threatened, they rarely resort to flight, but instead dive and swim away underwater or simply submerge slowly without a ripple and remain stationary with only the head showing, thus escaping detection while at the same time scrutinizing the danger. The striped chick can swim expertly shortly after hatching. To evade predators, it dives under floating vegetation and remains still, with only the bill exposed. Acting as a raft for the young, an adult submerges its hindquarters and allows the chicks to scramble aboard to seek the overhanging comfort of the slightly raised wings. Even when the parent dives, the young are not dislodged from their feathered submarine.

PLATE 3

Western Grebe

AECHMOPHORUS OCCIDENTALIS

Swimming together, the two grebes suddenly dove, to reappear moments later each holding a sodden mass of weeds in its bill. Their bodies held vertically, they emerged only halfway and faced each other with graceful necks outstretched and feet treading water. Slowly they approached, heads gently waving, until their breasts nearly touched. Then abruptly each flipped its burden aside and resumed normal floating posture.

Few birds exhibit such elaborate and spectacular courtship antics as the western grebe. That described above and pictured in the accompanying plate is termed the "penguin dance with weeds." Even more unusual is the "rushing ceremony." As if to warm up for the so-called race, two birds engage in mutual bill-dipping and head-shaking. Alternately they threat-point, a ritual that includes an enlarging of the throat, erection of the twin crests, and grotesque bulging of the scarlet eyes, all accompanied by vocal clicking and growling. Slowly the birds close on each other until almost touching. Abruptly, they make a right-angle turn and with their bodies vertical, necks strongly arched, and bills horizontal, dash madly across the water side by side, only their vigorously paddling feet touching the surface.

The western grebe is endemic to North America, breeding from portions of southwestern and south central Canada south to southwestern Minnesota, northwestern Nebraska, central Colorado, Utah, Nevada, and central California. It winters near the Pacific coast, largely on salt water, from southeastern Alaska to Jalisco.

On the breeding grounds it has two major requirements: a large area of open water for feeding, courting, and social flocking, and an adjacent expanse of emergent aquatic plants, such as cattails or tules, for nesting. The nest is a large stationary or floating mound of decayed and fresh aquatic weeds. Hundreds of closely spaced nests may be placed in a small area. The three or four eggs are pale bluish green or buff when freshly laid, but soon turn white, dark buff, or olive and usually become permanently stained by the browns of the wet nest material.

In the summer quarters the diet consists of small fish, insects, a few amphibians, and some vegetable matter. In the saline portions of its winter environment, where it congregates in flocks of hundreds or even thousands, the western grebe adds mollusks, crustaceans, and marine worms.

The western grebe, or "swan grebe," is the only member of its family (Podicipedidae) that has unstriped young. The chicks are fully clothed in a mouse-gray down—short, dense, velvety, and darker above than below. Demonstrating that there is still much to be learned about even our common birds, ornithologists recently discovered that this species is unique among our grebes in possessing two color phases. In typical dark phase (light phase shown in plate), the bill is dull greenish yellow; the black of the crown extends well below the level of the eyes; and the back, flanks, and hindneck are darker.

PLATE 4

Black-Footed Albatross

DIOMEDEA NIGRIPES

Through the dense fog, the far-off sound of pounding surf invaded the solitude of our tiny vessel, and the raucous cries of countless birds and the rank but exciting odor that characterize a large seabird colony assailed our senses. And there, shrouded in gray mist, the barren jagged rocks of Southeast Farallon Island loomed ahead. Breaking into the open, we were suddenly surrounded by a din of activity as myriads of rotund little auklets, bizarre puffins, and streamlined cormorants floated, dived, and buzzed around us. Hundreds of sparkling gulls hung overhead, and sea lions barked their greeting as we skirted the treacherous reefs. Scientists from the Point Reyes Bird Observatory, pursuing their lonely vigil as sole custodians and investigators of the island wildlife, waved as they recognized friendly visitors.

Our senses numbed, we resumed our westward path and soon entered the silent vastness of the open ocean. Suddenly, from the stern came the cry, "Albatross!" Fifty pairs of binoculars swung to the north, scanned the distant horizon, and focused on a dim speck as it sailed away. Immediately, the skipper stopped the engines, and as if in response, the bird executed an abrupt about-face and soared directly toward us, wheeling high over wave crests and skimming down out of sight into troughs on its seven-foot wingspan. Then it was upon us. Without a wingbeat, it circled the boat several times, settled majestically on the water only a few feet off the stern, and began to gobble up food scraps as fast as we could supply them. Out of nowhere a second bird appeared, and before long seventeen of these gigantic birds, almost within reach, groaned and squealed over the bonanza.

The black-footed albatross, or "black gooney" in mariner's vernacular, spends most of its life far out to sea, feeding on algae and all types of floating animal matter, including garbage from the ships that it follows for hours at a time. Confined to the North Pacific, it may be seen off the western United States throughout the year, although it is most common during its nonbreeding season, from July to late October. Nesting is now virtually confined to the Leeward chain of the Hawaiian Islands, where the species establishes dense colonies on exposed slopes or beaches. The single egg is dull white, sometimes marked with reddish brown, and is laid in a bare shallow depression in soil or sand. When the female lays an egg, she gently touches it all over with the tip of her bill, mutters a satisfied *ah ah ah*, and with a loud squawk settles contentedly upon it.

The courtship of albatrosses (family Diomedeidae) is humorous as well as spectacular. In the black-foot, two (sometimes as many as eight) birds stand face to face and alternately bow and fence or nibble with clacking bills. While one bird lifts the proximal portions of its wings and begins to preen, the other circles, points its bill skyward, stands on tiptoe, and turns its head from side to side, groaning and snapping its bill. Meanwhile, the first bird circles, snapping loudly. Finally, both bow formally, as if to compliment each other on a performance well done.

PLATE 5

Fork-Tailed Storm-Petrel

OCEANODROMA FURCATA

Two mysteries puzzled avian biologists for hundreds of years. The first began in 1667, when C. Comelin discovered nasal glands in water birds. For the next 265 years scientists described the occurrence, anatomy, and homologies of these organs. During that period, however, no one was able to determine their function, even when presented with the facts that marine birds have much larger nasal glands than do terrestrial species (so large that they leave deep grooves in the frontal bones of the skull) and that ducks raised in a salt-water environment have better developed glands than do members of the same species from freshwater habitats. In a 1932 monographic study, B. J. Marples concluded that the nasal glands produce a secretion that protects and cleanses the nasal lining, an erroneous theory that held sway for the next twenty-five years.

Meanwhile, scientists investigated a second mystery, concerning the methods by which marine birds could survive the ingestion of harmful sea water, a liquid with salt concentrations high enough to kill humans. Although field workers believed that pelagics, including storm-petrels, drank ocean water, physiologists claimed that they could not do so because the kidneys were too inefficient to remove the excess salts.

In 1957, K. Schmidt-Nielsen discovered that cormorants subjected to high loads of salt solution formed clear drops of liquid at the tips of their bills. An analysis of this secretion revealed amazingly high concentrations of sodium and chloride salts. Thus with one seemingly insignificant observation, two mysteries were solved: the nasal glands of marine birds function in concentrating and excreting harmful quantities of salts.

Although the salt glands of the present species have not been studied in detail, they presumably differ little from those of other members of the storm-petrel family, Hydrobatidae. Since the fork-tailed storm-petrel feeds largely on fish, crustaceans, and (reportedly) floating oil from dead or wounded marine mammals, it must ingest great quantities of salt water. The function of the elongated tubular nostrils in the order to which this species belongs—the Procellariiformes or "tubenoses"—is unknown, but may be related to the excretion of salts or to the great development of the olfactory sense.

This species breeds on coastal islands from northern California through the Aleutians to the Kuril Islands. During the winter it disperses to points both north and south, including southern California; some of the birds head to sea, where they sometimes form flocks of hundreds, whereas others seek sheltered coastal waterways.

The single egg is white, often with a wreath of dark speckles around the larger end. The typical nest is a shallow burrow in soil beneath trees or in the open. In a fork-tail colony the ground may become so honeycombed with tunnels that human visitors must stay away lest they break through and smash the nest contents.

PLATE 6

Pelagic Cormorant

PHALACROCORAX PELAGICUS

Most species of seabirds are colonial in their breeding habits. The pelagic cormorant, how-ever, does not seem to require the social stimulation or group protection afforded by the classical seabird colony, with its large size and closely packed nests. Choosing crevices or narrow ledges high up on precipitous cliffs overlooking the pounding ocean surf, pairs nest alone or with only a few neighbors. Although freed by inaccessibility from the depredations of most mammals, the nests are nevertheless subject to annihilation by winged marauders. Gulls and crows continuously patrol the periphery of colonies, waiting patiently to devour any unguarded egg or young. Simply by entering a seabird colony, a human intruder, no matter how careful and well intentioned, becomes an unwitting accessory to the crime by flushing the parent birds, thus exposing the nest contents to the mercy of avian predators.

The breeding range of the pelagic cormorant rings the northern Pacific Ocean from Japan north through Alaska and south to northern Baja California. The winter range is similar, but includes coasts slightly to the south on both continents and excludes the frozen wastes of Arctic seas.

The nest of this species may be used in successive years. With the annual addition of new materials—seaweed, grass, moss, and rubbish—the nest may attain a height of five or six feet. The three to five (rarely up to seven) eggs are pale bluish with a chalky coating. At hatching, the young resemble naked blackish grubs. Later they receive a coating of sooty down, which, however, does little to enhance their appearance.

So pigeon-toed are cormorants that they sometimes assume a comical stance with one foot atop the other. Such awkwardness on land results from structural adaptations for agil-ity in water, for it is here that these birds are at home. Leaping almost clear of the ocean sur-face, the cormorant describes an arching dive and, using its webbed feet for rapid under-water propulsion, torpedoes downward to depths of 500 feet in hot pursuit of crustaceans and small fish. Although pelagic cormorants usually feed alone, they are quick to take ad-vantage of food sources discovered by gulls or other species and hence may join the thou-sands of birds that sometimes compose a mixed feeding flock of seabirds.

During the winter the adults lose their nuptial adornments—the scattered white plumes on the head and neck, the white patches on the flanks, the twin crests, and the red color of the bare facial skin. The gular pouch is one of the structural characteristics that proclaim members of the cormorant family (Phalacrocoracidae) relatives of pelicans (Pelecanidae); both families are placed in the order Pelecaniformes.

PLATE 7

White-Faced Ibis

PLEGADIS CHIHI

The long decurved bill and wader's legs of the white-faced ibis are well adapted for feeding in shallow marshes and flooded fields, where these birds investigate crayfish holes and probe in the soft mud at the base of partially submerged vegetation. Almost any aquatic animal large enough to be worth the effort is fair game, from insects, leeches, mollusks, and earthworms to amphibians and small fish. Ibis may be identified almost as far away as they can be seen by their characteristic flight. With neck and legs outstretched and broad, rounded wings bowed downward, the bird alternates rapid series of flaps with short glides.

Like other members of its tongue-twisting family, the Threskiornithidae, this species is highly gregarious, not only feeding and roosting together but also breeding in colonies. A favored colony site in much of the West is an extensive and dense patch of tall tules. The rather deeply cupped nest is fashioned of old dead tules, lined with marsh grass, and placed near water level on a mat of the same vegetation. The three or four dull, pale greenish or bluish eggs are unmarked. Various species of herons and egrets may share the colony.

After an incubation period of twenty-one days, the eggs give forth young that resemble their parents only in their general shape and bare faces. They are covered, somewhat sparsely, with dull black down, relieved only by white patches on the throat and crown. Their feet are yellowish, and their elongated bills are pinkish flesh with black bands at the base, middle, and tip. The nestlings are fed by regurgitation from the crop of the adult, and the usual transfer method is reversed, with the young placing its bill into that of the parent.

Breeding today is confined largely to isolated colonies in a broad belt from northeastern California and southeastern Oregon east through southern Idaho, Nevada, Utah, and Colorado to Kansas; widely separated populations occur in northeastern Arkansas, the coasts of Louisiana and Texas, southern South America (thus paralleling the peculiar distribution of the cinnamon teal, *Anas cyanoptera*), and probably México. In the late summer, our United States birds engage in a postbreeding dispersal that carries them in all directions from their home marshes. This phenomenon, shared by most of our herons and egrets, has resulted in ibis sightings from all states west of the Mississippi River and from such far northern points as British Columbia and Alberta. In the fall the birds undertake a true migration to their wintering grounds. Most take up residence in México or on the coasts of Louisiana and Texas, but a few remain in central and southern California and, rarely, southern Arizona. One may witness in portions of our northern-bred human population a remarkably similar late summer dispersal, fall migration, and wintering behavior.

PLATE 8

Trumpeter Swan

OLOR BUCCINATOR

At one time the trumpeter swan bred from Alaska south through western Canada to Washington, Idaho, Wyoming, Nebraska, Missouri, and Indiana and wintered in such southern climes as North Carolina, Louisiana, Texas, northeastern Tamaulipas, and central California. But as man's conquest of North America advanced, the trumpeter retreated northwestward. Throughout the last century the feathers of the trumpeter and its close relative, the whistling swan (*Olor columbianus*), were in great commercial demand for quills, powder puffs, down, and adornments. Skins reached London markets by the thousands. In 1912, E. H. Forbush wrote: "The trumpeter has succumbed to incessant persecution in all parts of its range, and its total extinction is now only a matter of time. The trumpetings that were once heard over the breadth of a great continent . . . will soon be heard no more." In 1933 the United States breeding population numbered only sixty-six birds and was restricted to Yellowstone National Park and nearby areas such as Red Rock Lakes Refuge. Farther north, breeding was confined to a few scattered localities in Alberta, British Columbia, and probably Alaska. Finally alarmed by the species' imminent demise, the United States government afforded it rare and endangered status, thus entitling it to the most thorough management. As a result, the population level today stands at nearly 1,000 birds in the contiguous United States and perhaps three times that many in Alaska and Canada. Transplanting experiments are being undertaken to increase the breeding range.

The trumpeter swan is the largest member of the family Anatidae (ducks, geese, and swans). Its total length may reach six feet; wingspan, eight feet, two inches; and weight, thirty-eight pounds. Aside from an occasional small mollusk, crustacean, or insect larva, it feeds almost exclusively on the roots, tubers, and foliage of a variety of aquatic plants.

Despite its wide distribution geographically and in relation to life zones, the trumpeter is rather specialized in its requirements for breeding habitat. It needs bodies of fresh water that are shallow, quiet, and stable in level and that have marshy edges of sedge, cattail, or bulrush. The three to nine (average 5.1) off-white eggs are deposited on a platform of dead aquatic vegetation on a shoreline or mound. Muskrat (*Ondatra zibethica*) houses are favorite nest sites. The precocial downy young usually are mouse gray above and nearly white below. Rarely an all-white downy is produced, and a bird of this color phase molts directly into a solid white plumage rather than the usual grayish brown immature condition.

Although the species is generally quite wary, five young trumpeters visited Gwen Colwell at her meteorological station in British Columbia: "Peter, our goose, was fed his breakfast that morning on the ice ledge along the river bank. In no time the swans showed interest and soon . . . became so tame that they would scramble onto the ice when they saw us coming. At the end of the first week they had found their way to the house door. Upon several occasions we had all five huge birds in the telegraph office at once. They literally filled the room."

PLATE 9

Black Brant

BRANTA NIGRICANS

Despite its small size—hardly greater than a mallard (*Anas platyrhynchos*)—the black brant is the only common goose of western North America that inhabits the harsh marine environment. Breeding in the arctic maritime regions of eastern Asia, northern Alaska, and northwestern Canada, it migrates southward during the fall to winter along the Pacific coast from the southwestern corner of British Columbia to Baja California. Considered only a rare straggler inland, it frequents bays and estuaries, where it grazes on grassy mud flats or dabbles in floating kelp beds. On the wintering grounds its diet consists primarily of the leaves and roots of eel grass, with varying numbers of mollusks, crustaceans, and other small invertebrate animals.

The black brant's commitment to salt water extends even to its flight. The traditional wedge formation of other species of geese is replaced by a straight line perpendicular to the flight path. The flock flies close to the water; and when one member shifts up or down, the others follow suit one by one, producing a characteristic undulating motion within the line. So strong is their aversion to land that flying birds will usually avoid a land projection by neatly outlining the shore. In order to enter a lagoon, a flock has been known to fly several miles out of its way to utilize a narrow water passage rather than cross a sandbar a few hundred yards wide.

Although the black brant is a game bird, its diminutive size, wariness, and relative inaccessibility in its habitat make it much less sought after than its larger relatives. On its breeding grounds in Alaska, however, where the Norton Sound Eskimos refer to it as "luk-lug-u-nuk," it is a favorite quarry.

The nest, located on a marsh island or in a depression in tundra grass or moss near a lake, is composed solely of soft brant down, its color brownish flecked with white. The four to eight eggs are olive buff or creamy in color. While the female incubates, the short-necked male stands guard and defends his home vigorously against all intruders. When the adults leave the area temporarily, the female keeps the eggs warm and camouflaged by covering them with the nest feathers. Brant goslings are white and gray, rather than the usual yellow and brown of most other North American geese. As is true of all ducks, geese, and swans (family Anatidae), the young are precocial. This means that at hatching they are fully covered with down and are able to move about and feed themselves shortly thereafter. Some ornithologists merge *nigricans* with its eastern relative, the American brant (*B. bernicla*), a form very similar in coloration and habits.

PLATE 9

BLACK BRANT, *Branta nigricans*

Adult male; sexes similar
Length: 23-26 inches

PLATE 10

Ross' Goose

CHEN ROSSII

If the Hudson's Bay Company were to adopt an "official bird," it certainly should be the Ross' goose, for this species owes its discovery to Bernard R. Ross, a chief factor of that organization. At his insistence, the first specimens were obtained at Fort Resolution on Great Slave Lake in the Northwest Territories and were sent by Robert Kennicott to the Smithsonian Institution. The Smithsonian forwarded the birds to John Cassin of the Academy of Natural Sciences of Philadelphia, who named the species in 1861. But company involvement did not end there. Although the California wintering grounds soon became well known, the location of the breeding site remained a mystery. At the 1936 Presidential Wildlife Conference in Washington, D. C., sportsman-naturalist E. F. G. White induced Hudson's Bay's representative, R. H. G. Bonnycastle, to enlist the aid of his entire company. There followed four years of fruitless search. Finally, in the summer of 1940, Angus Gavin and Ernest Donovan, officials of the company, saw a single bird winging its way up the Perry River, well within the Arctic Circle on the south shore of Queen Maud Gulf in the Northwest Territories. Canoeing upstream, they became the first white men to set eyes on the nest of Ross' goose when they found a lake supporting about fifty breeding pairs. Fittingly, this discovery was first announced in *The Beaver*, a publication of the Hudson's Bay Company.

Since that time this species has been found breeding also on Southampton Island in Hudson Bay. It winters primarily in the marshes and fields of the Central Valley of California, where it feeds on old grain and tender new grass shoots. In recent years it has been increasing as a winterer on the gulf coasts of Louisiana and Texas. A favorite market bird in California, it dwindled steadily in numbers during the first part of this century, until in 1949 probably no more than 2,000 were left. With careful protection, however, it has recovered in recent years. In February of 1973, I observed a single flock of 1,500 of these sprightly geese near Gustine, California.

About the size of a mallard (*Anas platyrhynchos*), the Ross' goose (family Anatidae) is a miniature version of the white phase of the more familiar snow goose (*Chen caerulescens*), but possesses a bill that is much smaller, lacks the large black "grin" patch on the edges of the mandibles, and is adorned with tiny warty protuberances. The latter give the species one of its numerous nicknames, "scabby-nosed wavy." The call of the Ross' goose has been described as *luk-luk*, quite unlike the shrill *honk* of the snow goose.

As the explorers of the Hudson's Bay Company discovered, this species nests in loose colonies on islands in small tundra lakes. The nest is some twelve inches in diameter and composed of grass and down. The two to six eggs are creamy white. The down-covered young come in assorted colors; one brood of five contained two silvery white birds, one gray, one greenish yellow, and one bright yellow.

PLATE II

Cinnamon Teal

ANAS CYANOPTERA

Just as a person cannot wear the same shirt or coat indefinitely, so a bird cannot use the same feathers, for they would eventually become so abraded through contact with the nest, vegetation, and the elements that they could no longer function in protection, flight, or temperature regulation. Periodically (typically once or twice a year), the old feathers are replaced by the process of molt. Since a bird without feathers would be at a distinct disadvantage in coping with its environment, the feathers are molted usually a few at a time, so that at any given instant an individual will appear to have its full complement.

The male cinnamon teal, however, like the males of most members of the Anatidae, undergoes a peculiar summer molt, beginning in June and reaching its height in August, which eclipses the bright nuptial plumage in favor of a drab, femalelike aspect. During this process the large feathers of the wings are lost simultaneously, and the birds are rendered flightless for three or four weeks. Of little help in parental duties, these vulnerable males hide in heavy vegetation or, in the case of other species, flock to open water until flight is restored.

The cinnamon teal is the only pond duck that is restricted in its North American breeding range to the region west of the Mississippi River. It nests from southwestern Canada and Wyoming south to California, New Mexico, and México and winters from California and Texas south to northern South America. Additional populations occur in South America. Interestingly, our North American form was first discovered in Louisiana, where today it is of rare occurrence.

Quiet and inconspicuous, this teal rarely forms large flocks, preferring the solitude of pairs or family groups. It inhabits marshes and those shallow lakes and ponds that have emergent vegetation. In the usual manner of pond or dabbling ducks, it feeds by submerging its head and neck and tipping its body vertically, maintaining its position by vigorously paddling with its fully webbed toes. In this manner it procures tender sedges, pondweeds, and other vegetation, which provide 80 percent of its diet. The remaining 20 percent consists of animal food, primarily insects and mollusks.

When vying for the attentions of a female, swimming males sometimes play leapfrog, one bird rushing at another and jumping over him with flailing wings, in turn to be topped by his rival. At other times, floating before a female, a male will bob his head excitedly, an action that she occasionally returns. The typical nest, a depression in the ground, lined sparsely with grass and copiously with brown and white down from the body of the female, is carefully concealed in tall grass or herbage on rather dry ground, often far from water. The occasional nests that are located in marshes are built up above the high-water mark. The clutch size varies from six to fourteen, but is normally ten to twelve. The eggs are pale pinkish buff to pure white and are immaculate.

PLATE 12

Harlequin Duck

HISTRIONICUS HISTRIONICUS

Few birds are more aptly named than the harlequin duck. With its gaudy and seemingly haphazard pattern of blues, russets, black, and white, the male resembles the harlequin of old, the masked character of comedy and pantomime who wore multicolored tights. Indeed, both the generic and specific names of this bird, based on Latin, mean "relating to an actor."

A bit of an actor himself, the male harlequin courts his intended mate with genetically determined dialogue. Swimming around her with drooping wings, he suddenly throws back his head and points his gaping bill to the zenith. Then, jerking his head forward and downward, he utters a special cry. In the manner of most ducks (family Anatidae), the classic male chauvinists, the male of this species deserts his mate after the eggs are laid and consorts with the bachelors, immatures, and other derelict fathers.

Selecting a small island or point along a rushing mountain stream, the harlequin female builds her nest on the ground, either under a bush or in a crevice among rocks. Reports of nesting in hollow trees require confirmation. The nest itself is at first composed solely of grass, twigs, and leaves. After laying begins, however, the female plucks down from her body and places it around and under the eggs. The six or seven (occasionally five to ten) unmarked eggs are creamy, pale buff, or deep olive buff.

In North America the harlequin duck occurs in two widely separated populations. An eastern subspecies breeds from the coasts of Greenland and eastern Canada south to Labrador and winters from Labrador south to Long Island Sound. A western race nests from central western Alaska south through extreme western Canada to Colorado and central California and winters primarily along the Pacific coast from the Aleutians to central California.

During the summer, in their inland breeding localities, harlequins inhabit the most turbulent rivers. Sometimes the birds feed by wading in the shallows or, in slightly deeper water, by tipping up in the manner of dabbling ducks. Usually, however, they take to the tempestuous waters of midstream, where they maintain their position by rapid paddling. They invariably dive upstream into the current and when under water use both the feet and the half-folded wings for propulsion. Once the river bed is reached, the birds close their wings and walk along the bottom against the current, searching for food. Despite the swiftness of the water, they emerge close to the spot from which they dove, quite a feat for an animal that averages only one pound, seven ounces in weight. During the winter most individuals repair to the shores of the ocean, where they feed among surf-washed rocks in water usually less than twelve feet deep.

The harlequin duck is of little importance as a game bird. Its rough habitat and general rarity near population centers make it inaccessible to most hunters. Also, its normal diet of aquatic insects, crustaceans, mollusks, small fish, and tadpoles is said to make the flesh relatively unpalatable.

PLATE 13

California Condor

GYMNOGYPS CALIFORNIANUS

During the Ice Age, when sabertooth and mammoth roamed our continent and carrion was plentiful, vulturine species abounded. But with the evolutionary demise of many of the large mammals, vultures began to disappear, until today only the turkey vulture (*Cathartes aura*), black vulture (*Coragyps atratus*), and the rare California condor remain north of México. The extent of the condor's Pleistocene range suggests that this species was long ago doomed to extinction. In that period it inhabited such far-flung regions as Florida and Nuevo León. By several thousand years ago, well before Western man introduced his devastating culture, its range had shrunk to the area from British Columbia to Baja California and east to Nevada and Texas. Today breeding is confined to the Upper Sonoran life zone of the coastal mountains of California in a narrow strip 40 miles wide and 400 miles long from Santa Cruz County to San Diego County, with an isolated locality in Tulare County.

The reasons for this range reduction are obscure, but there can be little doubt that modern man has at least hastened the process through indiscriminate shooting, the use of poisoned predator bait, and simple disturbance of breeding sites. Now reduced to a total of only about fifty living individuals, the condor cannot survive without the immediate help of man. Since captive breeding does not appear feasible for this species, we must rely on the closure of nesting and roosting areas to human traffic and on full protection from killing.

One of the factors that dims hopes for recovery is the extremely low rate of reproduction. After an incubation period of forty-two days, the juvenile bird remains in the nest for five months, spends another two and a half flightless months near the nest, and is fed in part by the adults for an additional seven months. Sexual maturity is not reached until the age of about six years. Because an adult female lays only one egg every two years, the species could not survive were it not for the long life-span—one bird lived forty-five years in captivity.

The nest is a natural cavity, usually in a cliff or among boulders. The single pale greenish or bluish egg, irregularly covered with tiny pits and excrescences, is placed on a level padding of sand or silt. The egg may be up to 5⅜ inches long; one weighed 10½ ounces, and its shell held 9 fluid ounces of water—a fitting beginning for a bird that may reach a total length of 54 inches, a wingspan of 9 feet, 7 inches, and a weight of 31 pounds.

Sunning, the behavior depicted in the accompanying plate, is common to all members of the family Cathartidae. The function is not clearly understood, but probably concerns temperature regulation. Condors may sun up to twenty minutes at a stretch, particularly when the feathers are wet from a nocturnal rain or dew.

Ninety-five percent of the diet consists of dead cattle, sheep, horses, deer, and ground squirrels. There is no truth to the fable that California condors dispatch living animals; although their bills are powerful, their feet are more like those of a chicken in shape and have neither the strength nor the talons of a hawk or eagle.

PLATE 14

White-Tailed Kite

ELANUS LEUCURUS

Caught suddenly in the midst of a violent squall in the marshes near Alviso, California, my birding companions and I scurried to the shelter of our car, where we sat disconsolately staring through the rain-streaked windows. Almost immediately we became aware of another animal that had been affected by the storm. Perched nearby on the tiptop of a small tree was an adult white-tailed kite. With wings drooping and tail spread, the bird ruffled and shook its plumage, presenting the maximum feather surface to the pelting droplets. As the water began to penetrate, the feathers assumed a rather bedraggled appearance, which the bird was quick to rectify with preening motions of its hooked bill. Thus the rain, which was a nuisance to us as visitors, had provided a convenient bath for this denizen of the grasslands.

At one time a fairly common bird, by the 1920s the white-tailed kite had been extirpated from its range on the Atlantic coast of the United States and had been reduced to a few survivors in southern Texas, central California, and the east coast of México. In 1927 one author estimated that the largest stronghold—California—supported only fifty pairs, and scientists began to predict extinction for this beautiful species. During the 1950s and especially the 1960s, however, protected by law and, more effectively, by public enlightenment, the white-tailed kite began an amazing comeback. No longer the target for indiscriminate shooting, today it is spreading throughout Central America and has again become a common sight in parts of California.

The white-tailed kite inhabits grassy areas in agricultural bottomland, foothills, and marsh edges and places its bulky stick nest from three to fifty feet up in bushes and such trees as oaks, cottonwoods, willows, and eucalyptus. The three to five (rarely six) eggs are whitish, lightly to heavily scrawled with numerous shades of brown. While the female incubates, the male hunts for both. The male does not feed the young while they are small, but instead passes his booty to the female, either in the air or on a tree. In years of high rodent density, the female may build a second nest and incubate a new clutch while the male finishes raising the first brood. Unlike most members of its family (Accipitridae), this species is very social, forming winter roosts of up to 250 individuals and often nesting semi-colonially (one observer counted eighteen pairs in three square miles).

The food of this beneficial species consists almost exclusively of small rodents, with an occasional insect, snake, or small bird. When hunting, the white-tailed kite assumes a characteristic posture that has been termed *kiting*. Circling gracefully over a field, the bird suddenly pauses and begins to hover on slowly beating wings. Upon sighting a potential meal, it raises its wings into a sharp *V*, holds them motionless, dangles its legs, and slowly and quietly drops straight down upon its prey.

PLATE 14

WHITE-TAILED KITE, *Elanus leucurus*

Adult female; sexes similar
Length: 15-17 inches
California live oak, *Quercus agrifolia*

PLATE 15

Swainson's Hawk

BUTEO SWAINSONI

In the adult stage, most species of birds have but one plumage pattern. A few species, however, regularly exhibit genetically controlled color phases or morphs and are said to be polymorphic. Such a bird is the Swainson's hawk, a member of a family (Accipitridae) well known for its polymorphism. The typical light phase Swainson's hawk is brown above and whitish below with a brownish or rusty chest band. The dark phase is brownish black throughout, while the rufous phase is largely rusty on the underparts. All degrees of intermediacy occur, making field identification difficult even for an expert. Polymorphism should not be confused with such color abnormalities as albinism or melanism, which are the result of recurrent mutation.

This species has the longest migration of any North American hawk. It breeds in the prairies, farmlands, deserts, and other open spaces of the Great Plains and arid regions of the West from interior Alaska and northern Canada south to Texas and northern México. Each fall it congregates in huge flocks, numbering hundreds and sometimes thousands, and wends its way southward along the Middle American axis to winter primarily in the pampas of Argentina. During the return trip in spring, hundreds of birds may suddenly descend upon an open area, festooning scattered trees, bushes, utility poles, and even buildings or hopping about in grassy fields in search of their primary food—large grasshoppers and crickets.

Other fare includes frogs, lizards, snakes, and a variety of small rodents, some of which may be captured in the usual *Buteo* manner—a soaring search followed by a diving catch. The Swainson's hawk also employs aerial gyrations to snatch and eat large insects on the wing. The tameness of this hawk while perched atop a roadside utility pole, field hummock, or tree leads to its easy slaughter by undiscriminating gunners who know or care little about its totally beneficial habits. That the Swainson's rarely takes birds is amply demonstrated by the confidence with which smaller species treat this larger neighbor. The western kingbird (*Tyrannus verticalis*), house sparrow (*Passer domesticus*), and house finch (*Carpodacus mexicanus*) have all been known to construct their homes within the lower portions of the Swainson's bulky nest.

Choosing a tree with easy access and a wide view of the surrounding open terrain, the hawk places its nest from seven to 100 feet above the ground. Rarely, a large rock may be utilized as a nest support. The nest itself, composed largely of sticks, twigs, and grasses, is lined with bark, green leaves, lichens, and feathers. The two (rarely three or four) eggs are pale bluish white or greenish white and either immaculate or sparsely spotted with browns, grays, and buff.

PLATE 16

Harris' Hawk

PARABUTEO UNICINCTUS

With few exceptions, the basic bone structure of the hind limb of birds varies little from one species to another. Using the Harris' hawk as an example, we see that the toes number four, one less than in the primitive vertebrate condition. Like most species, the Harris' hawk stands on its toes, with the remainder of the "foot"—the bare tarsus, which is roughly homologous to the arch of the human foot—vertically inclined. In its elevated position, the ankle appears to be in the position of the human knee, until one realizes that this joint bends backward instead of forward. The true knee and the thigh are closely applied to the body and in the live bird are obscured by skin and feathers.

Modifications of the basic construction, both internal and external, are adaptations for different modes of existence. The Harris' hawk, for instance, shares with other members of its family (Accipitridae) toes that are long and widely spread and possess on their undersurfaces bulbous pads covered with small horny tubercules, adaptations of obvious value in catching and holding prey. The claws, which in raptors are called talons, are long, curved, and extremely sharp. Prey usually is dispatched by the crushing action of the powerful toes and by puncturing with the talons. The bill may be used to finish off the victim.

The Harris' hawk, like a number of raptorial species, is too tame and confiding for its own good and hence is less common and widespread than it used to be, at least in the United States. Formerly, it ranged into southeastern California and southern Louisiana and Mississippi. Today it is found from the southern portions of Texas and Arizona south through México and Central America to Argentina and central Chile. It is at home in semiarid grasslands interspersed with low riparian growth and thickets of mesquite and other thorny shrubs. Although it hunts mostly for rabbits and such rodents as wood rats and ground squirrels, it is not opposed to taking an occasional bird, which it plucks neatly before eating. That it also feeds on carrion has been postulated, but not proven.

The nest is a shallow platform of sticks placed from five to thirty (occasionally up to fifty) feet above the ground in a large yucca or cactus or in a low mesquite, hackberry, or cottonwood. The three to five eggs are dull white, sometimes faintly spotted with lavender, buff, or pale brown. When not incubating, the parent covers the eggs with vegetation.

Its easygoing nature unfortunately makes the Harris' hawk a favorite of falconers. To science and to its kindred, however, it renders a far more valuable service. Because it is easily bred in captivity, it is being used as a subject for carefully monitored studies on raptor reproduction. In the future, information from these experiments may be used in captive breeding of other hawk species now threatened with extinction. Individuals so bred may then be released into the wild to bolster natural populations.

HARRIS' HAWK, *Parabuteo unicinctus*

Adult male; sexes similar
Length: 17½-29 inches
Round-tailed ground squirrel, *Spermophilus tereticaudus*
Yucca, *Yucca angustissima*

PLATE 17

Prairie Falcon

FALCO MEXICANUS

Since time immemorial the soul of man has stirred to the sight of a falcon plummeting earthward in a powerful stoop or rocketing skyward in a towering ascent into the azure void. To watch a falcon settle on a windswept crag and survey its domain is to feel regal majesty and fierce independence, and to meet its piercing gaze is to feel a freedom that knows no bounds and is yielded to no master.

In falcons man senses the personification of such admirable qualities as deep pride, keenness of sense, and great physical power. Perhaps to atone for his own inadequacies or to bolster his own ego, man has within himself the innate desire to possess such an animal, to conquer and control it, to force it to do his bidding. For nearly 4,000 years the art of hawking, or falconry—"the sport of kings"—has been a favored and honored pastime, a hobby requiring great skill and patience. In recent years, however, with the realization that we are all animals, part of an ecological whole, and must strive to live together lest we perish, the practice of capturing and caging wild spirits has come under fire. In bygone eras falcons were plentiful, and "kings" were few. Hawk populations could withstand the pressure. Today our affluent society has brought falconry within the means of the average person. But this same culture, through injudicious application of pesticides, wanton destruction of habitat, and failure to rescind archaic bounty laws, has decimated hawk populations. The removal from the environment of even a single prairie falcon seriously threatens the existence of the species. Although falconry is still legal, it is now controlled by strict laws and hopefully will be banned within our lifetime. Because of man himself, because of his deleterious effects upon the environment and his changing ideals, the sport of falconry has become untenable. Unless ecological balance can be regained and hawk populations can return to their original levels, falconry must perforce become an interesting but undesirable anachronism.

The prairie falcon (family Falconidae) breeds in arid lowlands and foothills from southwestern Canada and western North Dakota south to northern Texas and northwestern México. During the winter it descends to lower elevations and extends its range into central México. The nest, located on a protected ledge or in a shallow hollow some thirty-five feet up on the face of an isolated cliff, consists of a slight scrape in the ground or the remains of an old nest of another species. An eyrie may be used year after year, although usually by different adults. The four or five (occasionally three or six) eggs are white or pinkish white with heavy blotches and spots of purple, browns, and cinnamon. This relatively large clutch size helps to offset the 74 percent mortality experienced by the young during their first year.

The diet varies from pair to pair, but usually consists of rodents and birds, the latter taken both on the ground and in the air. The capture of such species as the very fast white-throated swift (*Aeronautes saxatalis*), the large Franklin's gull (*Larus pipixcan*), and the wary black-billed magpie (*Pica pica*) attests to the hunting prowess of the prairie falcon.

PLATE 17

PRAIRIE FALCON, *Falco mexicanus*

Adult male; sexes similar
Length: 17-20 inches
Common flicker, *Colaptes auratus*

PLATE 18

White-Tailed Ptarmigan

LAGOPUS LEUCURUS

The white-tailed ptarmigan is the only North American bird species that is restricted throughout the year to the harsh environment of alpine tundra. Even during the short summer, icy winds sweep the exposed ridges, and driving rains and blustery snows penetrate the rocky crevices. Patches of winter snow linger in the darker recesses of the newly emerged rock fields, and nocturnal temperatures dip below freezing. White-tailed ptarmigan favor moist mossy outcrops where heath and dwarf willow are less than eighteen inches tall and scattered rocks, six to twenty-four inches in diameter, provide ample shelter from predators and the elements.

Ptarmigan, or "snow grouse," are well adapted to their rigorous life. The toes are flattened, completely feathered, and adorned with scaly lateral projections—a combination that produces effective snowshoes. The plumages are a classic example of protective coloration. When the mountains are shrouded in winter white, the birds are garbed completely in gleaming white. Come spring, the snows melt and the birds molt. By the time dark tundra vegetation and lichen-covered rocks appear, the birds have assumed a dark plumage: the upperparts, throat, and central (upper) rectrices are finely vermiculated with buff, white, and black; and the breast and flanks are white with bold black bars. Since in open terrain any movement is easily detected by predators, when threatened the birds freeze in position, often near a similarly colored stone, and let their disguise fade them to invisibility. So tame do ptarmigan become, where not hunted by man, that I was once able to touch the tail of a bird before it skittered away.

This cryptic coloration is of great advantage to the incubating female, for the nest is situated on open tundra, without concealing benefit of rock or bush. The nest is a simple depression lined with fine dried grass stems, feathers, and small leaves. The three to nine eggs (average 5.2 in Montana) are buff rather evenly covered with small spots of browns.

Each male establishes and defends a territory, but departs by the time of hatching, leaving to the female the domestic chores of raising the precocial chicks. Although males are occasionally polygamous, the women's liberation movement could do little for this species, for females have considerable freedom of their own. One coquet nested a quarter mile from the territory of her mate, was seen with a different male each of the two succeeding years, but nested on the territory of her first mate the third year.

Adult ptarmigan (family Tetraonidae) are grazers. The winter diet consists largely of the buds and twigs of dwarf willow, alder, and birch. During the warm months, other foods are added: moss; grass stems; and the leaves, flowers, and fruits of a variety of plants.

The white-tailed ptarmigan ranges from central Alaska, northern Yukon, and southwestern Mackenzie south to the Kenai Peninsula, Vancouver Island, the Cascade Mountains of Washington, and along the Rockies from British Columbia and Alberta to northern New Mexico.

WHITE-TAILED PTARMIGAN, *Lagopus leucurus*

Adult male in breeding plumage; sexes similar

Length: 12-13 inches

Alpine willow, *Salix anglorum* var. *antiplasta*

PLATE 19

Sage Grouse

CENTROCERCUS UROPHASIANUS

The crisp clear air lay still over the sagebrush hills. Patches of snow lingered in dark shelterings, and the sparse brown grass stood brittle with evening frost. Even before the first faint glow illuminated the eastern horizon, the male sage grouse began to congregate on their ancestral strutting ground. First one arrived, then several, until nearly fifty cocks dotted the barren flat. Nearby, inconspicuous in the bordering vegetation, the hens appraised the first contestants as they initiated the time-honored ritual. Standing very erect, with tail cocked and spread and wings held slightly away from his body and almost perpendicular to the ground, a male inflated the twin, greenish yellow air sacs until his whole neck and breast were greatly distended and his black belly nearly hidden. Then with sudden backward jerks of his head, he raised the resonating sacs high, drew in the skin between them, and expelled air from his throat to produce the so-called drum, a very deep and soft *punk-de-punk-punk*.

These intricate courtship displays, typical of the family (Tetraonidae), begin in February and continue into May. Such an assembly of birds is termed a *lek*. Although at times one cock will dash at a rival, contact fighting rarely ensues. Thus the ritualistic courtship not only attracts females, so that mating can be consummated, but also serves to avoid injurious fighting, so that the males may later face the rigors of their environment in a healthy condition.

Except for the turkey (*Meleagris gallopavo*), the sage grouse, discovered by Lewis and Clark, is the largest upland game bird in North America. Male grouse are said to attain a weight of eight pounds and females five pounds. Compared to the male, the shorter-tailed female has a light chin, less black on the belly, and lacks the stiff white ruff and bright air sacs. True to its name, this grouse is restricted in range to the sage-covered spaces of the Great Basin of the western United States and adjacent Canada, where it occurs from 4,000 to 11,500 feet in elevation. Populations are essentially resident, although vertical migration during the winter sometimes takes birds as much as 100 miles from their summer quarters. The sage grouse is primarily a browser, existing most of the year on leaves, buds, and berries, together with a small quantity of seeds. Leaves of the sagebrush are particularly favored, in some areas providing nearly all the sustenance during winter. In spring and summer various insects are also consumed.

The nest, located on the ground beneath a sheltering bush, usually sage, consists of a slight depression sometimes lined with grass or twigs. The seven or eight large eggs are greenish drab, evenly spotted with various shades of brown. The female alone cares for the single annual brood, while the polygamous males join each other in a carefree life unencumbered by family responsibilities.

SAGE GROUSE, *Centrocercus urophasianus*

Adult male in breeding plumage courting
Length: Male 26-30 inches

PLATE 20

California Quail

LOPHORTYX CALIFORNICUS

Although many members of the family Phasianidae are polygamous, the male California quail is a proper homebody, mating with but a single female and helping in the care and protection of the family. Upon hatching, the precocial young are clothed in a variegated pattern of fluffy down—yellow, black, white, and russet. Within a short time they can run expertly, and after some ten days they attain a set of miniature flight feathers with which they are able to flutter short distances.

Despite this mobility and the protection afforded by the parents, the chicks are subject to a great deal of predation. Such animals as snakes, skunks, foxes, crows, and jays exact their toll. Contrary to popular opinion, however, most hawks and owls are not major predators on quail. Those unenlightened game managers who indiscriminately gun down birds of prey are only doing themselves and their charges a disservice, for these species actually benefit the quail by eliminating rodents that raid nests or compete for food. Modern biologists even advocate that game farms maintain nest boxes for barn owls (*Tyto alba*), one of which may take hundreds of rodents in a year while never molesting a quail.

Other factors add to the high mortality in quail. The nest, lined with leaves and grass, is placed in a depression on the ground and hence is an easy mark for any foraging mammal or reptile that might stumble (or slither) upon it. The habitat—brushy growth in agricultural land, rangeland, or desert—while affording ample cover for retreat, also provides a home and convenient approach screen for numerous enemies. To help offset this high rate of attrition, the California quail lays a large number of eggs, usually ten to seventeen in a clutch, thus increasing the odds that at least a few young will reach maturity. The creamy or whitish eggs are well disguised with irregular blotches of brown. Behavioral characteristics also protect the quail. The winter flocks, while engrossed in the search for seeds, small fruits, foliage, buds, and invertebrate animals, are carefully guarded by sentries perched alertly atop a bush or hummock. When the danger alarm is sounded, and if running is not the solution, the birds burst from the underbrush with such a startling whir of wings that the would-be predator becomes confused and is unable to make a catch.

Originally, the range of the California quail extended from southwestern Oregon, northern California, and western Nevada south to southern Baja California. Today, although less common in total numbers, the species is more widespread owing to extensive introductions, even in such far-flung regions as New Zealand and Hawaii. So well did the species take in some areas that a Sonoma, California, game farm, needing new stock, was able to import birds from Chile!

The female is not always particular as to where she deposits her eggs. In one instance, a quail laid two eggs in the nest of a yellow-breasted chat (*Icteria virens*). After the chat added its fourth egg, the two birds took turns incubating.

PLATE 21

Mountain Quail

OREORTYX PICTUS

Charles Schulz's cartoon character Pigpen, the little boy who seems to move in a perpetual cloud of dirt, should be reincarnated as a mountain quail. Like other members of its family (Phasianidae), this species never bathes in water, but cleans its feathers by dusting. A variety of dusting methods are used by birds. Generally, a bird squats or lies on soft dry earth and employs bill-pecking, foot-scraping, body-shuffling, and wing-flicking to create a cloud of dust that filters into the plumage, later to be expelled with vigorous body shakes. The precise functions of this behavior are not clear; probably, ectoparasites are dislodged or the feathers somehow conditioned. Whether or not Pigpen derives some benefit from his protective coating, only Charles Schulz knows.

The mountain quail, or "plumed partridge," occurs from about 1,500 to 10,000 feet in elevation from southern Washington and southwestern Idaho to northern Baja California. It has been introduced on Vancouver Island and in the western portions of Washington and Colorado. Diverse habitats are utilized: dense undergrowth of coastal redwood forests; mountainous pine-oak woodland; and hillsides and canyons clothed with chaparral plants such as manzanita, chinquapin, and snowbush. One race inhabits the sage-pinyon-juniper association. A prerequisite for breeding is a nearby supply of free water, which is required by chicks soon after hatching. This dependence on water was clearly demonstrated in August of 1947, when several thousand birds congregated at the only available source, Jackass Spring in the Panamint Mountains of California.

In mountainous country, where winter snows cover the food supply, individuals form flocks and undergo a vertical migration to lower elevations, proceeding entirely on foot and often in single file, their two-feathered crests cocked backward at a pert forty-five degree angle. These winter coveys disperse only during the breeding season, when pairs establish nesting territories. The male advertises his presence with a loud, clear, whistled *quee-ark*, which can be heard three-quarters of a mile away. The nest, a ground hollow lined with leaves, pine needles, grass, and quail feathers, is well concealed by bushes, grass, or an overhanging log, rock, or bank. The eggs are pale reddish buff and average between nine and ten to a clutch. The twenty-two eggs discovered in two layers in a single nest probably were the product of two females.

Mountain quail feed primarily in the early morning and again in the evening. Ninety-seven percent of their diet consists of grain, weed seeds, fruit, and such assorted vegetable material as flowers, buds, leaves, pine seeds, and grass bulbs. Animal food includes centipedes and a variety of insects. The flesh is said to be unusually palatable, and during the last century birds brought $2.50 to $4.00 per dozen in the San Francisco market.

PLATE 22

Black Oystercatcher

HAEMATOPUS BACHMANI

Catching an oyster or mussel, animals not known for their quickness, should not be much of a chore for an oystercatcher, and indeed it is not. At one time scientists believed that the bird simply inserted the tip of its laterally compressed bill and severed the adductor muscles that hold closed the two valves of a mollusk. Recent careful studies, however, have shown the process to be somewhat more complicated. Walking over wave-swept ocean rocks, the oystercatcher searches diligently for a mussel that is resting with its valves slightly open. Spying a gaping shell, the bird uses its square-tipped bill to deliver a sharp blow to the dorsal border of the mollusk. This strike depresses the valve and causes a permanent abnormal gap. With a series of jerks, the bill is driven into the gap and used as a crowbar to wedge the shell open, in the process often fracturing the left valve. The leverage applied by oystercatchers is so invariably left-handed that it produces asymmetry of the left portion of the adult skull. After the valves are separated, the bird uses its bill like a pair of scissors to snip the flesh away from the shell. An expert oystercatcher may accomplish this entire feat in a matter of seconds and is capable of consuming some 200 mussels per hour.

Oystercatchers also eat many sandworms, crustaceans, chitons, and barnacles. Small limpets are often ingested whole and their shells regurgitated in the form of pellets. Frequently, birds carry their prizes to a favorite dining rock, which after a time may become cluttered with hundreds of empty shells.

The black oystercatcher is restricted in range to the rocky shores of the Pacific coast from the Aleutians south to west central Baja California. So well does the black plumage blend with the dark hues of the rocks that only the bright red bill or penetrating whistles betray the bird's presence. When an adult sounds the alarm, the chicks instantly crouch and freeze until danger has passed. This lack of motion, together with the protective coloration of their fluffy down, sooty tipped with light buff, makes the young almost invisible among the rocks. Meanwhile, the parents attempt to divert the intruder by running away in a semi-crouched position with the feathers of the nape raised and ruffled and the tail spread.

The nest takes a variety of forms, but usually consists of a rock depression laboriously lined with small stones and located just above spray level on an islet, reef, or shingle beach. The two or three (rarely one or up to five) eggs are creamy buff, rather evenly spotted and scrawled with black and dark browns.

Oystercatchers, of which only six species are recognized, belong to the same order (Charadriiformes) as the plovers, sandpipers, gulls, and alcids, but because of their numerous structural peculiarities are relegated to their own family, the Haematopodidae.

PLATE 23

Long-Billed Curlew

NUMENIUS AMERICANUS

For shorebirds such as the long-billed curlew, which nests in exposed situations in open terrain, problems of maintaining secrecy from predators are paramount. Rather than build a readily visible nest atop the ground, the female (and male?) curlew fashions a shallow depression termed a *scrape* and lines it inconspicuously with bits of the surrounding vegetation, notably grass and lichens. The eggs, usually numbering three or four in a clutch, are well camouflaged, being whitish buff to light greenish olive or brownish olive in ground color, sparsely to thickly blotched with dark umber, chocolate, and olive. So that no conspicuous curlew outline appears against the horizon, the incubating adult (either sex) extends its bill, head, and neck and crouches close to the ground, relying on its marbled buff and black plumage for protection. Such behavior assumes great importance when one considers the length of the incubation period: twenty-seven days and fourteen hours ($\pm$ nine hours). After leaving the nest, the precocial chicks respond instinctively to the warning cries of the adults by melting into the grass, crouching, and freezing until the "all clear" is sounded. Meanwhile the parents employ a "broken-wing act," a distraction display designed to decoy away possible predators. To gain the attention of a predator, the curlew simulates injury. Flopping along the ground, dragging its wings and tail, the bird stays barely out of reach of its pursuer. A. C. Bent once saw a long-billed curlew lead a hungry coyote fully half a mile before they disappeared over a hill.

The long-billed curlew (family Scolopacidae) breeds on dry prairies and moist meadowland from the southern portions of British Columbia, Alberta, Saskatchewan, and Manitoba south to Texas, New Mexico, and Utah. Formerly it bred as far east as Illinois, but today farms there have severely reduced the available habitat. Evidence indicates that breeding is compatible with cattle grazing. The species winters from California, western Nevada, Texas, and Louisiana south to Guatemala and sparingly along the Atlantic coast from South Carolina to Florida. At this season it seeks food on mud flats, open marshes, grassy fields, sandbars, and beaches. An opportunistic feeder, it is known to take berries, worms, snails, crustaceans, spiders, insects, frogs, and even nestling birds.

The poorly described nuptial flight apparently involves two birds that glide and call together over the prairies. Adults have eight different calls, perhaps the commonest of which is a loud, clear *curl-e-e-e-u-u-u*, rising in the middle and then trailing off.

Straight and stubby at hatching, the bill grows quickly and, when mature, becomes one of the noblest in the animal kingdom, reaching an amazing eight and three-quarters inches in length. Its uses have not been clearly elucidated, but probably it is advantageous in probing the tunnels of aquatic worms. Long-billed curlews have been known to defend their territories aggressively even against Swainson's hawks (*Buteo swainsoni*). The bill, although of little use as a weapon, could have some value as an instrument of intimidation.

LONG-BILLED CURLEW, *Numenius americanus*

Adult female on nest with juveniles; sexes similar
Length: 20-26 inches

PLATE 24

Black Turnstone

ARENARIA MELANOCEPHALA

Our surprisingly woeful ignorance of the biology of those bird species restricted to western North America is clearly illustrated by the black turnstone. In two large bibliographies on shorebirds, I was unable to find a single reference to this species. Further search revealed only a few minor papers since the 1929 publication of A. C. Bent's *Life Histories of North American Shore Birds* (U. S. National Museum Bulletin 146). Only sketchy descriptions, leaving much to be desired, are available on its calls, courtship, incubation, and food habits, and apparently there are no data at all on the care of the chicks. Its recent transferral from the family Charadriidae to the Scolopacidae indicates the sad state of our knowledge of its taxonomy. Yet in winter the black turnstone is a common sight along the Pacific coast from southeastern Alaska to Baja California and the gulf shores of central Sonora. It breeds exclusively, but commonly, on the mainland coast and nearby islands of Alaska, from Cape Prince of Wales on the Seward Peninsula south to Chichagof Island, all easily accessible areas.

The display flight of the male is said to include a strange *ʒum-ʒum-ʒum* noise similar to that made by air passing through the stiffened outer tail feathers of a courting common snipe (*Capella gallinago*). However, neither the wing nor tail feathers of the turnstone seem to be structurally modified for sound production. Little or no attempt is made at lining the nest, which is simply a depression in matted dead grass, usually near a pool margin or on an islet. The four eggs are peculiar in the faintness of their markings; the almost lusterless, yellowish olive ground color is only faintly marked with spots and splotches of two darker shades of brownish olive.

During the winter this species frequents the intertidal zone of rocky coastal promontories and, to a lesser extent, mud flats and gravelly or kelp-littered beaches. Here it apparently feeds on a variety of small marine invertebrates. It is quite gregarious, associating not only with its own kind, but with surfbirds (*Aphriza virgata*) and rock sandpipers (*Calidris ptilocnemis*) as well.

The name *turnstone* is derived from the peculiar feeding habit of overturning or pushing aside pebbles, kelp, and other debris to uncover food. The upturned bill is especially well suited for this behavior. When an object is too heavy to be moved by a simple thrusting motion of the head, the bird steps back a bit and gets a running start, using its bill as a battering ram. Still larger objects are said to be moved by several birds working in unison. With so many interesting facets to its biology, the black turnstone certainly deserves more attention.

PLATE 25

Surfbird

APHRIZA VIRGATA

Despite its abundance and wide range, the surfbird remains even today somewhat of an ornithological enigma. The generic name, *Aphriza*, comes from two Greek words, *aphros*, meaning "sea foam," and *ʒao*, meaning "I live"—apt terminology for a species that winters almost exclusively on surf-pounded coastal rocks. The nest went undiscovered until 1926 and, when finally found, was not in the littoral environment, where explorers had searched for years, but several hundred miles from the coast, high above timberline in the alpine tundra of the barren, rugged mountains of south central Alaska. The birds arrive at or near the breeding grounds in late May and begin departing in late July. Thus the non-breeding season, which is spent along the Pacific coast from southeastern Alaska to the Strait of Magellan, lasts ten months. Those individuals that winter in southern South America travel some 24,000 miles during the year, one of the longest of bird migrations.

The courtship behavior, often quite spectacular in shorebirds, is undescribed, as are many other aspects of the breeding biology. The few breeding birds that have been found favored the windy summits of lichen-covered rockslides, with short, scant growth of grass, moss, and other vegetation—a habitat corresponding exactly with that of Dall's sheep (*Ovis dalli*). The nest is completely exposed on dry rocky ground and is composed of a natural erosion depression lined with bits of dry moss, lichens, and dead leaves of *Dryas integrifolia*, a member of the rose family. The four eggs are buffy with profuse spots and splashes of fawn and bay, tending to concentrate as a wreath encircling the large end. Although only the male has been observed on the nest, probably both sexes incubate, as both have a brood patch—a heavily vascularized area of thickened, featherless skin in the abdominal region that facilitates the transfer of heat from the parent to the eggs. The surfbird has a peculiar distraction display. When a Dall's sheep or human approaches the nest, the sitting bird remains quiet until the very last second, then suddenly explodes upward into the face of the intruder, forcing a retreat. This behavior perhaps evolved to prevent the accidental trampling of the eggs.

The food habits are also poorly known. The summer diet apparently consists of about 91 percent beetles and flies, which are actively pursued over the rocky terrain. During the winter, the surfbird feeds largely in the intertidal zone of rocky shores. Mussels, limpets, barnacles, and small periwinkles are taken.

For years ornithologists have argued over the proper familial relationships of the surfbird. Until quite recently, it was placed in the plover family, Charadriidae. Currently it resides with the more typical shorebirds in the family Scolopacidae. The problem will not be resolved until we learn a great deal more about this mysterious species.

PLATE 26

American Avocet

RECURVIROSTRA AMERICANA

To a functional anatomist, a peculiar anatomical structure suggests an equally strange action. In the case of the American avocet, the strongly upturned bill functions in an unusual feeding behavior. Wading in shallow water, a bird submerges its head until the convexity of the bill touches the soft bottom mud. Then, with the mandibles slightly open, it lopes along, swinging its head from one side to the other with each step. Apparently depending on the sense of touch, the bird instantly seizes and eats any tender morsel that passes between the mandibles. A dozen or more birds may line up in formation and cross a pond in unison, each doubtless deriving benefit by procuring items dislodged by its cohorts. At other times, avocets pick at the surface of the water or mud or dash headlong after flying insects. Seeds of marsh and aquatic plants, small fish and mollusks, shrimp and other crustaceans, and a variety of insects, both adult and larval, are taken.

The recurved bill gives rise to the name of the family, Recurvirostridae, a group containing seven species, only two of which occur on the North American continent. During the summer, the American avocet inhabits meadow ponds, open shallow marshland, and the muddy borders of alkaline lakes from southwestern Canada south to Texas, northern México, and southern California. It winters in similar habitats and on coastal mud flats from central California and southern Texas south to Guatemala.

The avocet is semicolonial in its breeding habits. Nests are placed in a variety of exposed situations, such as gravelly islands, sparsely grassed dikes, and the dry caked mud of alkaline flats. Scratching with their feet, the adults form a shallow scrape and line it (if at all) with materials such as marsh grass or mud chips collected within a few yards of the nest site. In areas subject to flooding, the nest may be built up as high as fifteen inches. The two to four eggs (average 3.7 in Oregon), which are olive buff, blotched and spotted with black and browns, hatch after an incubation period of twenty-four days. The precocial chicks are able to vacate the nest an hour later. They are competent swimmers and when hard-pressed can even dive. Like the adults, they often feed by tipping up in shallow water in the manner of dabbling ducks.

This species is exceptional in maintaining three different territorial arrangements according to the particular stage of its breeding cycle, which lasts from seventy-one to eighty-six days. During the prenesting period, both members of a pair defend, against other avocets, a territory centered around a feeding site. After incubation begins, a secondary foraging area, embracing the nest, is also guarded; defense is much less effective, however, because most of the time one member of the pair must remain on the eggs. After the hatching, the territory centers on the chicks and is therefore somewhat mobile; during this period, defense is directed not only toward other avocets, but toward differing species as well.

PLATE 26

AMERICAN AVOCET, *Recurvirostra americana*

Adult male in breeding plumage; sexes similar
Length: 15½-20 inches

PLATE 27

California Gull

LARUS CALIFORNICUS

In 1848 the Mormon settlements bordering Great Salt Lake were invaded by vast numbers of hungry black "crickets" that threatened to destroy the crops on which the pioneers depended. When hope was nearly lost, a few California gulls appeared over the horizon, and soon thousands joined the feast, devouring the pests and miraculously saving the harvest. To commemorate the event, the grateful Mormons erected a monument to the gulls and designated the species the Utah State bird.

The timely arrival of the gulls was certainly fortunate, but hardly a miracle, for they nest in colonies of hundreds and even thousands on nearby Great Salt Lake. Not very particular in their eating habits, these birds are quick to take advantage of any newly available food supply, so that their diet varies from month to month and from one locality to another. In Utah 53 percent of the diet consists of grasshoppers of the family Locustidae. In one day in 1947, a flock of 8,000 gulls consumed an estimated 154,472 grasshoppers. The Mormon cricket (*Anabrus simplex*), actually a long-horned grasshopper of the family Tettigoniidae, hatches in spring and thus enters into the diet soon after the gulls arrive from their winter quarters. California gulls also feed on carrion, earthworms, fish, amphibians, birds and birds' eggs, small rodents, grain, strawberries, cherries, and numerous other insects, including beetles, flies, cicadas, and damselflies. A large contingent of gulls can always be found at the local garbage dump.

California gulls breed from Great Slave Lake, Canada, south to Mono Lake, California, and from Klamath Lake, Oregon, east to Stump Lake, North Dakota. From these interior localities, they migrate in a westerly direction to winter along the Pacific coast from British Columbia south at least to Colima, México. In California they abound in city parks, where they wait confidingly for handouts, and will follow fishing boats for miles into the ocean. During the day they often roost on moored boats and city buildings. Like many gulls (family Laridae), the California gull does not attain its mature plumage until the spring of its fifth summer, when almost four years old. Most immatures spend the summer on the wintering grounds, although a few breed during their fourth summer.

The nesting colonies are located on or near the shores of low-lying islands in marshes and freshwater or saline lakes. The nest is placed on the ground or among rocks at least two or three feet from the nearest neighbor. The territory around the nest is jealously guarded against the encroachment of other adults and their precocial young. The nests are rather large structures, generally fourteen to eighteen inches in diameter, and are fashioned from dead weeds, sticks, grass, and feathers. The two or three eggs vary considerably in ground color and markings; often they are buffy brown or smoke gray, rather evenly decorated with small, highly irregular spots of brown and gray.

PLATE 28

Franklin's Gull

LARUS PIPIXCAN

Stray chicks of most gull species are accepted by only their own parents and often are severely beaten or killed by the other colonists. A lost Franklin's gull downy young, on the other hand, may find refuge and a permanent home in any nest upon which it chances during its wanderings. Some adults actually accumulate young, sallying forth to round up passing strays until ten or a dozen overflow the nest. The young are, however, supposed to remain home, and many adult "bird-hours" are expended containing and admonishing the venturesome types. A swimming chick wind-drifted away from the colony is anxiously driven back by a cloud of vociferous adults, which, when necessary, may resort to lifting the downy ball by the nape and hurling it shoreward.

The Franklin's gull (family Laridae) breeds from southeastern Alaska south through the Canadian prairies to Oregon, Utah, South Dakota, Iowa, and Minnesota. It forms vast colonies of up to 30,000 birds along reedy lake margins and in marshes, often in association with the eared grebe (*Podiceps nigricollis*), black tern (*Chlidonias niger*), and yellow-headed blackbird (*Xanthocephalus xanthocephalus*). Using dead bulrushes, the gulls fashion a floating platform two or three feet across and attached to standing plants. Then they add a more delicate superstructure, four to twelve inches above the water, to form the nest proper. The two or three eggs are some shade of buff or greenish buff, heavily to lightly marked with spots, blotches, and scrawls of browns. An abrupt rise in water level sometimes dislodges nests from their reedy moorings. Left to the mercy of the winds, they drift freely until, touching a favorable shore, they are once again anchored by the faithful parents. Because of the vagaries of the weather, marshes that are suitable one year may be dry or flooded the next, causing the birds to be somewhat nomadic in colony location.

Early each morning the Franklin's gulls, or "prairie doves," stream out in all directions from the colony to spend the day feeding on the surrounding plains and farms. Together with California gulls (*Larus californicus*) and ring-billed gulls (*L. delawarensis*), they form an exquisite cloud behind a plow. Dropping one by one to the freshly turned furrows, these birds waddle along until the immediate supply of upturned insect larvae has been exhausted, and then leapfrog ahead to take up position near the tractor, where the gleaning is more lucrative. They also eat spiders, water beetles, and grasshoppers, and the stomach of one specimen contained 327 dragonfly nymphs. Adept flycatchers, these beneficial birds swirl to great heights in pursuit of flying midges.

During the fall adults lose the pink breast, bright soft-part colors, and most of the black head, retaining only a dusky patch extending from eye to eye around the rear crown. In preparation for their long migration, they congregate in immense flocks and wander over the prairies in search of suitable feeding sites. Most of the population winters on the Pacific coasts of Peru and Chile.

FRANKLIN'S GULL, *Larus pipixcan*

Adult male in breeding plumage on nest with juveniles; sexes similar
Length: 13½-15½ inches

PLATE 29

Heermann's Gull

LARUS HEERMANNI

Because bird guides must be small enough to carry easily into the field, they cannot treat all the atypical or intermediate color variations found among birds. The beginning birder, therefore, soon encounters confusing birds that do not match his field guide plates or text. A case in point is the Heermann's gull. In the normal adult, the upper wing coverts are solid deep gray, and the primaries are black. In an occasional individual, however, each wing has, near its bend, a white patch, which varies from extensive and solid to small and piebald. Although a rare condition, it is persistent within the population and can be observed with regularity on the coast of California.

The limited breeding range of the Heermann's gull embraces the Revillagigedo, Tres Marietas, and Tres Marías islands, San Roque Island on the west coast of Baja California, various islands in the Gulf of California, and a few rocks near the coasts of Sinaloa and Nayarit. The largest breeding colony, numbering in the tens of thousands, is on Raza Island, a wildlife refuge in the Gulf of California. The gulls arrive in late March, quickly claim the level terrain, and establish territories eighteen inches to several feet apart. As a rule, the nest is a well-formed, unlined scrape in sand or among rocks. In some localities the nest is a compact structure of sticks, weeds, dry grass, and feathers. The two or three eggs, among the handsomest in the gull family (Laridae), are some shade of grayish, marked with lavender, grayish brown, grayish blue, and umber.

In July the birds leave the nesting colonies and wander north to southern British Columbia and south along the Pacific shores of México. In late summer and fall they are abundant on the coast of California. Some birds winter north to Oregon and south rarely to Guatemala, but by January the bulk of the population is concentrated in southern California and Baja California.

Largely a coastal fisherman, the Heermann's gull sails up behind an unsuspecting school of herring, dips quickly to the surface, and submerges its bill or entire head to grab a meal. It also works kelp beds and the intertidal zone to obtain mollusks, shrimp, and other crustaceans. Although less of a scavenger than the larger members of its genus, it will at times visit garbage dumps.

Much like jaegers, this species pursues and harries boobies, terns, and other gulls into dropping their catches. The Heermann's gull specializes in robbing brown pelicans (*Pelecanus occidentalis*). When a pelican plunges into the ocean and bobs up with a netful of fish, it finds one or two gulls floating expectantly within reach. As the pelican attempts to swallow its prey, the gull grasps any exposed part of a fish and drags it out of the pouch. In one such encounter, a gull thrust its whole head into the pouch, whereupon the pelican clamped down hard. The two struggled for half a minute until the hapless gull finally extricated itself, minus a few feathers, but willing to try again.

PLATE 30

Elegant Tern

THALASSEUS ELEGANS

Each spring on Raza Island in the Gulf of California, a fascinating interaction takes place between the Heermann's gulls (*Larus heermanni*) and the elegant and royal (*Thalasseus maximus*) terns. The gulls arrive first from their winter quarters and by late March or early April, when the terns begin to appear, have established territories covering the choicest flats of the island. One night when the tern population has swelled sufficiently, several thousand screaming birds swirl over a portion of the gull colony, drop to the ground en masse, and by sheer numbers force the gulls to abandon their nests and move aside. Initially about twenty feet across, this round, embryonic tern colony shrinks during the next day as the gulls at the periphery snatch up any unguarded eggs and the robbery victims leave to try an twenty-five or thirty feet in diameter. Because nocturnal expansion exceeds diurnal contraction, the tern colony soon reaches its maximum size, about one acre. Later in the season, there appears in the center of the tern colony an empty space tightly ringed by the downy chicks that hatched in the earliest and now abandoned nests. The gulls are quick to occupy this void, and thus the tern colony dwindles from within just as it had previously enlarged around its circumference.

Strictly a coastal marine species, the elegant tern breeds along the Pacific side of Baja California at Scammon Lagoon and San Roque Island and in the Gulf of California on Raza, Trinidad, and George islands. In late summer and fall it wanders north to northern California and south along the Pacific coast of México. It winters on the coasts of Peru and Chile. In California it was formerly considered an erratic straggler, occurring only from August to October. In 1951, however, approximately 1,100 birds appeared in Los Angeles County, and in 1954 some 1,500 were counted in San Diego County. July and November records became numerous. In San Diego the sighting of two breeding-plumage adults on June 18, 1955, prompted Burt L. Monroe, Jr., to predict future breeding, and in 1959 local birders there discovered a colony of thirty-one nests, the first for the United States.

The nest of the elegant tern is a simple bare scrape in sand, positioned about nine inches from its neighbors, a distance that slightly exceeds the bill reach of the two incubating adults. The one or two eggs are whitish or pale pinkish buff, boldly marked with irregular blotches of violet gray and various hues of the darker browns.

Although terns are placed in the same family (Laridae) as gulls, their feeding behavior is quite different. Gulls descend to the surface of the water on open wings, feet first. The elegant tern seeks small fish by circling and hovering two to ten feet above the water and then executing a headlong dive that nearly carries it beneath the surface.

PLATE 31

Marbled Murrelet

BRACHYRAMPHUS MARMORATUS

Unquestionably, the greatest unsolved mystery in American field ornithology today is the whereabouts of the nest of the marbled murrelet. Records of the search date back to 1842, but despite abundant clues, no one has been able to conquer this stubborn holdout. At first the quest centered on the immediate coasts of the mainland and adjacent islands, where many members of the family Alcidae nest in ground burrows or rock crevices. On May 23, 1897, in the Prince of Wales Archipelago, Alaska, G. G. Cantwell collected an adult female murrelet. In its oviduct he discovered an egg, pale chalcedony yellow, lightly and uniformly peppered with small spots of blackish brown. Since then, several other eggs have been found in the same manner.

When in 1918 a flightless juvenile murrelet was picked up on the floor of an Oregon forest twenty-five miles from the coast along the south fork of the Coos River, attention shifted inland. In June of 1931 a nest purportedly of this species was discovered among rocks in the mountains of Chichagof Island, Alaska, but recently the identity of the parents has been seriously questioned. Another fledgling was found as it floated down Pescadero Creek in the Santa Cruz Mountains of central California, fully ten miles from the seashore; still others have been noted in forest situations far removed even from streams. In the evening, adults are frequently observed buzzing inland like huge brown bumblebees. During nighttime, and especially at dusk and dawn, this bird's sharp *keer, keer, keer* has been heard repeatedly high among the misty treetops of the redwood forests of California. That its summer range matches almost exactly the distribution of coastal coniferous forests probably is no coincidence. Thus the evidence for forest nesting seems indisputable.

That no nest has been accidentally discovered in the well-populated parks frequented by these birds suggests that the exact site is not on or in the readily accessible ground but hidden high in the 200-foot trees. Indian legend depicts a chubby bird with an uptilted bill perched on a redwood bough near a crude nest. Perhaps this is more fact than fancy. In 1970, chagrined by the elusiveness of this nestless wonder, the editors of *Audubon Field Notes* (24:264) offered $100 for the first thoroughly documented occurrence. So far no one has claimed the reward.

The marbled murrelet feeds both in placid coastal waterways and rough ocean tide rips, usually within a few hundred yards of shore. The few dietary data available indicate that it concerns itself primarily with small fish and to a lesser extent with mollusks and crustaceans.

An Asiatic race of this species is found from Kamchatka to Japan. During the summer our North American subspecies occurs (and presumably breeds!) along the Pacific shores from Unalaska and Kodiak to central California. It winters from southern Alaska, and casually farther north, to southern California. Its abundance on the coasts of British Columbia and Alaska makes even more remarkable our inability to discover the nest.

PLATE 32

Tufted Puffin

LUNDA CIRRHATA

Cursing under his breath, the fisherman rebaited his hook once more and cast it into the dark water. And yet again he felt the gentle tug and the slight slackening of his line as the hook's burden was stealthily removed. Popping buoyantly to the surface, the "sea parrot" eyed its host and waited patiently for its next free meal. But the fisherman was not to be robbed again. Setting his oars, he shot forward, cut sharply across the bow of an oncoming boat, and thus switched the feathered pest to another luckless angler.

Although sometimes taking advantage of such a convenient food supply, the tufted puffin usually does its own fishing. Diving expertly, it half opens its wings in the manner of other alcids (family Alcidae) and virtually flies through the water in swift pursuit of small fish. When not thus engaged, the puffin streaks to the bottom and searches out a spiny sea urchin or hard-shelled mollusk.

The tufted puffin is restricted in range to the northern Pacific, breeding as far south along the coast as southern California. Strictly an oceanic species, or pelagic, it comes to shore only to breed and even then prefers coastal islands to mainland sites. The two adults, identical in appearance, choose a handy crevice on a rocky slope or use their sharp nails to dig a three- to four-foot-long burrow in soft earth. On some islands the ground may become so honeycombed with tunnels that a person can scarcely walk without falling through upon a hapless puffin. The tufted puffin lays only one egg per clutch and hence may be severely threatened by any upset to the natural balance of its breeding cycle. The egg is pale bluish white or dull white, often obscurely marked with scrawls of violet gray and pale brown. After about twenty-one days of incubation, in which both parents share, the eggs hatch into tiny powder puffs of slaty black down. Like most pelagics, the young gorge themselves on the parents' offerings until they become quite obese. They remain in the burrow until fully feathered and able to fend for themselves at sea.

The brightly colored bill and long ivory tufts of the adults presumably function in courtship. During the fall molt, the white face is lost, and the tufts are reduced to a mere suggestion of their former elegance. The plates that form much of the length and about one-third of the height of the huge bill are also shed each fall, to be replaced the next spring in preparation for the breeding season.

When not engrossed in parental duties or feeding far out at sea, the adults stand sentinel at the entrance to the burrow. Although comical in appearance, these white-faced clowns with their grotesque orange noses maintain a solemn and dignified demeanor and habitual silence, which engenders admiration and some envy in those of us lucky enough to visit the rocky domain of the "old-man-of-the-sea."

PLATE 33

Band-Tailed Pigeon

COLUMBA FASCIATA

Although often relegated to the status of an old wives' tale, pigeon milk really does exist and apparently is common to all members of the family Columbidae, to which the band-tailed pigeon belongs. During the last few days of incubation, in the adults of both sexes, cells in the lining of the crop swell and begin to slough off, carrying their milky contents. The milk, a thick whitish fluid that looks and smells much like cheese, is fed to the nestlings by regurgitation and provides their only sustenance in the first few days of life. Although rather similar in composition to mammalian milk, being rich in both proteins and fats, pigeon milk lacks calcium and carbohydrates. When the young grow older, they are fed a combination of milk and whatever hard foods the adults can glean from their environment. Adult food consists almost exclusively of nuts and berries. These are swallowed whole and repose for a time in the two-chambered crop (an extension of the esophagus), which may become so distended as to produce a grotesque bulge on the side of the neck.

A very swift and direct flyer, the band-tailed pigeon is nevertheless capable of amazingly acrobatic twists, turns, and drops when threatened. These characteristics, together with the palatability of the flesh, make this species an excellent game bird. As a result, during the latter part of the nineteenth century, populations in the United States nearly succumbed to hunting pressures. In the nick of time careful studies revealed that, like its less fortunate relative, the passenger pigeon (*Ectopistes migratorius*), the band-tailed pigeon usually lays only one egg and attempts only one brood per year. It is a biological axiom that in order to maintain itself, a species must produce as many offspring as there are fatalities. With each successful *pair* producing only a single young annually, the lowest reproductive rate of any North American game bird, unlimited hunting seriously affected the total population. With few natural enemies, the band-tailed pigeon had evolved a delicately balanced behavioral pattern that could be upset only by the modern technology of man. Fortunately, careful governmental regulation of hunting seasons allowed the species to recoup its losses, so that today it is again a common inhabitant of pine-oak forests from British Columbia, Utah, and northern Colorado south to Nicaragua.

The white egg is deposited on a low horizontal tree limb on a frail platform of coarse dried twigs, which may number as few as sixteen and which are so loosely arranged that the large interspaces would seem precarious for the eggs. The unusual courtship display of the male must be irresistible to the female. Bending horizontally on a tree branch, he inflates his neck and swings his bowed head from side to side. Then, with tail depressed and fully spread, he stretches his head upward and emits an enticing *coo*. At other times he launches skyward. Soaring in a semicircle, with neck outstretched and wings and tail spread, he utters a peculiar chirping sound; and after a rapid shallow fluttering of his wings, he descends to his perch.

PLATE 34

Inca Dove

SCARDAFELLA INCA

When nest-building, the female Inca dove perches at the nest site and arranges the materials brought by the male. The presentation is highly ritualistic. Alighting near his mate, the male walks to her, climbs onto the midscapular region of her back, and passes the material toward her side. The end result, completed in about three consecutive days, is a small, rather loose platform of sticks, with a shallow but definite cup lined with grasses. Some pairs fashion weak "false" nests, which are abandoned before construction begins on the final version. The nest is placed from four to twenty-five feet up in a bush or tree. One couple utilized a fern basket along the corridor of an occupied ranch house.

So that the two white eggs are never left uncovered during the thirteen- to fourteen-day incubation period, the parents take turns in attendance, the male in the middle of the day and the female the remainder of the time. Throughout the nestling period, which lasts fourteen to sixteen days, the feces and excrement of the young infiltrate the nest materials and act as an adhesive to form a more rigid and substantial structure. Frequently, nests thus strengthened are relined and used to raise subsequent families; one nest was used for four successive years and housed eleven broods. This unusual process of cementation and reuse probably is of great value in reducing egg and nestling mortality, for the reinforced nest can better withstand the destructive elements of the environment.

In the breeding season the Inca dove is highly aggressive in its territoriality, a circumstance that poses some problems for a species in which the plumages of the sexes are virtually identical. The sexes recognize each other by their responses to certain ritual behavior. Head-bobbing, for instance, is initiated by a male and returned only by females. A male thus accosted simply ignores the error in judgment, or if things go too far, actively shrugs off his pursuer. A male displays to his mate by assuming a horizontal attitude one or two feet away, elevating and fanning his tail, and uttering a soft throaty *cut-cut-ca-doah*. A similar call, an excited *cut-cut-cut-ca-doah*, is used territorially against intruding Incas. Perhaps the most commonly heard of the four calls in the repertory of this species is a soft mournful *coo-coo*, which serves primarily as an advertisement and is so often repeated as to be nerve-rackingly monotonous.

This species, like other members of its family, Columbidae, is highly social and almost totally nonaggressive when not breeding. Birds rest, sun, and feed together, sometimes in flocks of over 100. So chummy do they become that at night one may roost on the back of another!

The Inca dove is a permanent resident in arid tropical and arid subtropical regions from southern Arizona, New Mexico, southern Texas, and Tamaulipas south to Costa Rica. In portions of the tropics, and even to some extent in south Texas, it breeds throughout the year. In choice of habitat, it prefers villages and modified urban parkland, where it takes a variety of small seeds from the ground surface.

PLATE 35

Roadrunner

GEOCOCCYX CALIFORNIANUS

It was with considerable excitement and anticipation that my two birding companions and I approached Mesquite Spring, an isolated patch of trees at the northern extremity of Death Valley National Monument. Here we hoped to find one of the various species of eastern vagrants that for some unknown reason veer widely from their normal migratory pathways and enter the desolate wastelands of eastern California. Almost immediately we discovered a female orchard oriole (*Icterus spurius*), a very rare visitor and the first I had ever seen in the state. After feeding in the trees for several minutes, the oriole flew to the ground and disappeared into a dense patch of weeds. As we approached to obtain a better view, a roadrunner abruptly appeared over the crest of a nearby hill and walked stealthily down the slope toward us. Suddenly it crouched and then plunged headlong into the weeds. Instantly a frenzied screech issued from the undergrowth, and a second later the wily roadrunner emerged grasping the terror-stricken oriole in its bill! Immediately giving chase, I bounded over hill and cactus, but soon discovered that catching such a fleet-footed rascal is no mean feat. Fortunately, the roadrunner soon abandoned its prospective meal and with an indignant wave of its tail vanished into the desert. When I reached the victim, it was lying on its back and panting heavily. Although badly winded and shaken, it was unhurt and soon recovered enough to be released into the trees, much the wiser for its harrowing experience.

The usual diet of the roadrunner consists of large insects, scorpions, tarantulas, and similar invertebrates, but it will not decline a tasty lizard or a small mammal or snake. Neither is its bird-catching propensity abnormal, for several bird species, including the house sparrow (*Passer domesticus*), mockingbird (*Mimus polyglottos*), and even a swift, captured in midflight, have been recorded as prey. Although its speed has been exaggerated in popular cartoons, the roadrunner has been clocked at fifteen miles per hour and is probably capable of an even faster gait, for it can soon outdistance the average human.

The roadrunner is resident in deserts and arid woodlands from northern California, Nevada, Utah, Colorado, southwestern Kansas, and parts of Oklahoma, Arkansas, and Louisiana south to central México. This species is a member of the cuckoo family (Cuculidae) and thus is closely related to the European cuckoo, which gave its name and voice to our familiar cuckoo clock. However, unlike its European relative, which lays its eggs in the nests of other species, the roadrunner builds its own home, a bulky structure about a foot in diameter and positioned from three to fifteen feet up in a thorny bush, mesquite, or dense clump of cactus. The two to six eggs are white, overlain with a chalky or yellowish film. The typical spring song, a descending series of rather loud, hoarse *coos*, begins with the bird's bill nearly touching the ground and ends with it pointed toward the sky. Thus the roadrunner has been described as starting with its head low and coo high, and ending vice versa.

PLATE 35

ROADRUNNER, *Geococcyx californianus*

Adult male; sexes similar
Length: 20-24 inches
Barrel cactus, *Echinocactus acanthodes*

PLATE 36

Pygmy Owl

GLAUCIDIUM GNOMA

In most species of birds, the male is larger than the female. Within the family Strigidae, the typical owls, however, this sexual dimorphism is reversed, females usually weighing more and having longer wing lengths than males. Although a number of hypotheses have been advanced to explain this phenomenon, no conclusions have yet been reached. The theory that currently holds sway states that size dimorphism reduces competition for food between the members of a mated pair. The female pygmy owl, which averages some eleven grams heavier, takes fewer birds and more mammals than her smaller mate. Probably, her larger size provides more effective striking power in handling mammals, but less maneuverability for catching birds. Thus by concentrating on different foods, the mates avoid extreme competition and are able to coexist within a small territory, with its limited resources, without eating themselves out of house and home. Comparison of the various species of owls reveals that those that feed on large prey items, such as rodents and birds, exhibit greater sexual dimorphism in size than those that utilize small and numerically abundant prey, such as insects and other invertebrates. Thus, where competition would be greatest, evolution has favored the selection of increased size dimorphism.

The pygmy owl occurs in coniferous forests, aspen groves, oak stands, and mixed woods throughout western North America from southeastern Alaska and northern British Columbia south through the Rocky Mountains and California to Guatemala. It prefers edge situations, and early in the morning may be discovered perched atop a dead snag with tail cocked at a rakish angle and breast bared to the warm sunlight. Although abroad at all hours, it is most active at dawn and dusk. Its commonest call is a monotonous series of musical hoots repeated at the rate of one note per one or several seconds. If the observer is well hidden, a whistled imitation may produce startling results by attracting a vigilant pygmy. Even if no owl appears, the imitator may be mobbed by a variety of small woodland birds come to scold the potential predator.

Each pair of pygmy owls occupies a large feeding territory. Hardly bigger than a bluebird, the pygmy can lick its weight in wildcats, attacking and dispatching ground squirrels twice its size. It concentrates, however, on mice, lizards, grasshoppers, and beetles, with an occasional small bird for variety.

Like most small owls, the pygmy utilizes abandoned woodpecker holes or natural tree hollows in which to nest. The three or four white eggs are nearly round, averaging only three millimeters longer than wide.

PYGMY OWL, *Glaucidium gnoma*

Adult female; sexes similar
Length: 7-7½ inches
California black oak, *Quercus kelloggii*

PLATE 37

Elf Owl

MICRATHENE WHITNEYI

Members of the family Strigidae, the typical owls, have a number of structural adaptations for their largely nocturnal activity. The eyes, for instance, are widely spaced and frontally directed—attributes that produce binocular vision and hence excellent depth perception. The reader may test the importance of depth perception by closing one eye and reaching quickly for various objects. More often than not his hand will fall short. An owl must execute quick strikes at darting mice in darkness and has few good chances per night. A significant number of misses could well result in starvation for the owl or its dependent offspring.

The eyes of owls are fixed in bony sockets and cannot be rotated in the manner of the human eye. To compensate for this inability and for the narrow field of view that results from the frontal direction of the eyes, owls have evolved anatomical peculiarities that allow them to twist the entire head over 180 degrees. Another attribute, the sharp visual acuity of owls, is well known and is of obvious advantage in hunting under conditions of poor illumination. Some owls are able to see in one-hundredth the amount of light required by the human eye. In total darkness, however, owls are just as blind as the rest of us.

As one might expect in a bird that makes its living during darkness, owls have excellent hearing. In addition to possessing an auditory sensitivity that corresponds to their own rather low voices, owls are able to detect the high squeakings of rodents. Many species of owls have large ear openings bordered anteriorly by a fleshy erectile flap, which probably functions like the cupped hand held in front of one's ear to intensify sounds coming from the rear. Such an arrangement aids not only in hearing prey, but also in detecting predators while the owl is looking the other way. In some species the ears are asymmetrical in size and position—an adaptation for pinpointing the direction of prey sounds.

The elf owl, the smallest owl in the world, is almost entirely insectivorous, feeding largely on crickets, noctuid moths, and scarab beetles. It also takes scorpions, neatly removing the poisonous tail tip before ingestion. Never drinking free water, this tiny terror obtains all it needs from its juicy food.

The elf owl breeds from southeastern California and the southern portions of Arizona, New Mexico, and Texas south into México. In winter it leaves the United States to take up residence in southern México. Although best known as an inhabitant of saguaro-cactus desert, it breeds wherever ample insects and proper nest sites are available, from mesquite flats and riparian growth of cottonwood and walnut to pine-oak woodland up to 7,000 feet in elevation.

The nest, located from seventeen to sixty feet up in a tree or giant cactus, consists almost exclusively of an abandoned woodpecker hole. The two or three (rarely one or up to five) white eggs are laid on the bare floor of the cavity, without benefit of a lining. Incubation, performed solely by the female, is completed in twenty-four days. Meanwhile, the male hunts for both members of the pair and warns away rivals with a call consisting of five or more notes delivered endlessly and sounding much like the yapping of a puppy.

PLATE 37

ELF OWL, *Micrathene whitneyi*

Adult female; sexes similar
Length: 5-6 inches
Saguaro cactus, *Cereus giganteus*

PLATE 38

Burrowing Owl

SPEOTYTO CUNICULARIA

Ask the average person for his mental image of a typical owl (family Strigidae), and he will describe a solitary bird that nests in trees, sleeps during the day, and spends the night ghosting through the forest in pursuit of mice. Although many of our North American owls, such as the spotted (*Strix occidentalis*) and great horned (*Bubo virginianus*), fit this mold, *Speotyto* does not.

Shunning forested areas, the burrowing owl inhabits flat, rather arid plains and prairies from sea level to some 9,000 feet in elevation. Where natural terrain is lacking, it utilizes pastureland or the artificial confines of airports and even golf courses. A widespread species, it breeds from southwestern and south central Canada south through the western United States to Tierra del Fuego. Isolated populations occur in Florida, the Bahamas, and the West Indies. When winter approaches, it migrates from the more northern reaches of the Great Basin and Great Plains and extends into portions of the southeastern United States.

As its name implies, the burrowing owl lives in holes in the ground. Some evidence suggests that these birds sometimes dig their own burrows, but no one has ever documented the feat. Instead, the members of a pair locate an abandoned mammal hole, such as that of a ground squirrel or fox, and renovate it with powerful backward scratches of their feet. Unlike the nests of most birds, the burrowing owl's abode serves not only for breeding, but also for roosting, food storage, shelter, and retreat from enemies. The six to twelve (commonly seven to nine) white eggs are deposited on a nest lining of grass, feathers, and, in some localities, dry chips of horse or cow dung. Shortly after the young hatch, the lining is completely removed. Unusual items found at the entrances to burrows include rags, a woolen mitten, charcoal, dry corncobs, and bits of hide and bone.

Behaviorally, this species can hardly be considered a typical owl. Perhaps because of its dependence on mammal digs, it frequently is colonial. In addition to being nocturnal, it is diurnal and crepuscular. Preceding copulation and while singing, the male courts his mate with a "white and tall performance" (see plate), in which he assumes an erect stretched posture and exposes the white regions of his throat and eyebrows. Occasionally, the male presents the female with a gift, such as an insect or choice toad. In addition to the primary song, a long series of cuckoolike notes with the second syllable drawn out, the extremely varied vocal repertory includes a chatter, rasp, scream, whine, grunt, warble, rattlesnake call, and chuck, the last delivered with an abrupt bow.

The diet is composed of crickets, grasshoppers, beetles, dragonflies, scorpions, toads, lizards, a variety of small mammals, and an occasional small bird. Ground foraging is the most common method of feeding. Resembling an American robin (*Turdus migratorius*) in this activity, a burrowing owl runs along the ground, pauses, then dashes ahead, or sometimes flies, to capture its prey. Fly-catching, hovering, and searching from an elevated perch are other hunting methods employed.

PLATE 38

BURROWING OWL, *Speotyto cunicularia*

Adult male courting; sexes similar
Length: 9-11 inches

PLATE 39

Spotted Owl

STRIX OCCIDENTALIS

Many species of owls, especially during the nonbreeding period, choose a favorite perch, where they roost, singly or in small flocks, over a long period of time. If one is lucky enough to discover such a spot, he will find, littering the ground, the remains of many a day's meal, neatly cast in rounded gray pellets. After an owl swallows a small mammal, be it a mouse, shrew, or ground squirrel, the digestive processes remove all but the hair and bone, which are then regurgitated in the form of a pellet. Usually, one pellet equals one meal. Pellets are our most important source of information on the food habits of owls. A pellet analysis is a commendable project for school children and for those adults who do not realize the beneficial nature of our birds of prey. Open a few pellets in front of a farmer, and he will soon be eager to protect the owl roosting in his barn. To discover the contents of a pellet, first soften it in water, then carefully dissect out the fragile bones and wash them off. They will come out clean and white. Skulls often remain intact, and, together with the toothed lower jaw, are the most useful portions of the skeleton for both the identification and counting of prey items.

The spotted owl is one of the least frequently observed of all North American owls and apparently is nowhere common. One of its major requirements seems to be absence of sunlight, for it inhabits only dense forests and, in the Southwest, deep, heavily shaded canyons. Ranging from sea level to 9,500 feet in elevation, it resides in three primary areas: the Pacific coast region from southwestern British Columbia south along the Cascades and coast ranges to central California, the southern Rocky Mountains from central Colorado to northwestern México, and the Sierra Nevada and southern mountains of California.

Entirely nocturnal, it feeds on rodents, bats, flying squirrels, shrews, moles, amphibians, and large insects. Included among the few birds that are taken is the tiny pygmy owl (*Glaucidium gnoma*). Often the only clue to its presence is a loud *hoo, hoo-hoo, hoo-o-o*, at a distance resembling the bark of a dog. Like the closely related barred owl (*Strix varia*) of eastern North America, the spotted has a variety of other calls, including a spine-tingling whistle, raspy, high-pitched, and inflected. During the day, this species perches on a low bough and becomes exceedingly tame, often allowing close approach and sometimes even capture by hand—a gloved hand!

The bulky nest has been found in a variety of sites, including abandoned bird nests, tree cavities, cliff potholes, and rocky shelves at the entrances to caves. The two or three (rarely four) eggs are white, like those of all members of its family (Strigidae).

PLATE 40

Poor-Will

PHALAENOPTILUS NUTTALLII

In the eighteenth century, barn swallows (*Hirundo rustica*) were believed to pass the winter buried in the mud at the bottom of ponds. Since that myth was shattered by the discovery of migration, several species have been proven to exhibit torpidity. None, however, was known to hibernate until, on December 29, 1946, Edmund C. Jaeger discovered a comatose poor-will wedged into a shallow niche in a granite boulder in the Chuckwalla Mountains of southern California. Attempts to rouse the bird by shouting and handling evoked little response; it simply lazily opened and shut one eye. Ten days later the bird was still in its "crypt." When picked up, it emitted several "puffy" sounds and a variety of high-pitched whines, opened its mouth as if to yawn, and then resumed its rest. Further manipulation prompted the bird to raise both wings to a rigid, fully outstretched vertical position, which was maintained for several minutes. Later the same day, the bird was again taken from its roost, but this time it suddenly awoke and flew away. The next year a poor-will was retrieved from the same crevice and banded. It remained for three weeks and returned the subsequent winter.

The poor-will (family Caprimulgidae) breeds from south central British Columbia and northwestern South Dakota south to central México. A crepuscular species, it perches on exposed ground and flops into the air to snatch flying insects—a living to which it is admirably suited by virtue of its cavernous gape. Where winter colds decimate insect populations, however, such a diet is disadvantageous; and most northern poor-wills are forced to migrate, wintering from central California, southern Arizona, and southern Texas southward. Because migration is a hazardous and energetically straining undertaking, great benefit accrues to any bird that can survive winter perils in another manner. Apparently, rather than culling out those individuals that failed to move to warmer climates, selection in the poor-will favored the evolution of the physiological state of hibernation. Laboratory studies have shown that hibernation in this species is triggered by a supply of food insufficient to support activity in cold weather. During hibernation the heart and respiratory rates decline drastically; and body temperature, normally 95–110.3°F, may drop as low as 40.6°F. It has been estimated that on an equal amount of fat, a dormant bird can conserve enough energy to live ten times longer than an active bird.

Poor-wills inhabit low open forests, brushy deserts, and rocky foothill canyons in arid and semiarid country from below sea level to nearly 10,000 feet. Squatting on the ground, as is its usual wont, this bird becomes virtually invisible among leaf litter and pinecones. As it will not flush until nearly stepped upon, often the only clue to its presence is its melancholy whistle, *poor-will-ip*, the middle segment accented and the last audible only at close range. Making no attempt to build a nest, the poor-will deposits its two faintly pinkish eggs in a slight depression on bare ground, rock, or matted pine needles, usually beneath the edge of a small bush or tuft of grass.

POOR-WILL, *Phalaenoptilus nuttallii*

Adult male; sexes similar
Length: 7-8½ inches
Single-leaf pinyon pine, *Pinus monophylla* (cones)

PLATE 41

White-Throated Swift

AERONAUTES SAXATALIS

Sitting on the steep grassy hillside, amid golden poppies and azure lupines, lazily surveying the panoramic view of the San Francisco Bay area, I was lulled by the warm morning sun and the sound of gently pounding surf below. Suddenly, my silent reverie was split by a loud, high-pitched, excited twitter, and I found myself ducking involuntarily as a pair of white-throated swifts dashed past my ear so close that I could both hear and feel the rush of air from their wings. Down into the valley they dived, their strident *tee-dee, dee, dee, dee* echoing behind. Then they were back, shooting upward into the void, their cigar-shaped bodies twisting and turning in great aerial gyrations. As suddenly as they had appeared, they sped behind a hill and were lost to sight and sound, leaving in their wake an impressed and breathless observer.

The white-throated swift (family Apodidae) is thoroughly committed to an aerial existence, and few birds can match its abilities in flight. It is said to be able to escape a stooping peregrine falcon (*Falco peregrinus*) at speeds exceeding 200 miles per hour. It never perches on vegetation or the ground, but courts, feeds, and even obtains nesting materials while on the wing. To drink or bathe, it drops low and momentarily skims the surface of a pond or river. Even copulation, when not accomplished at the nest site, takes place in the air, one bird engaging another and the two pinwheeling downward for as much as 500 feet.

The tiny bill belies the huge gape, which is used as a net to ensnare airborne insects such as beetles, leafhoppers, wasps, winged ants, and especially flies. When cold weather reduces insect abundance, this species is able to survive temporary periods of fasting by conserving energy in a state of torpor, during which the body temperature, normally 96.1–105.8°F, may drop as low as 68°F without ill effects.

In the evening, white-throated swifts flock into crevices high in the virtually inaccessible walls of precipitous rocky cliffs. As if to take aim on the tiny entrance to their nocturnal roosting cavity, the birds swirl around for some time, making numerous false passes. Finally, they take the plunge almost in unison, occasionally colliding with each other in their apparent frenzy.

The nests are placed in similar situations, frequently in colonies. Composed primarily of feathers, often with some grass or plant down, the simple cup is securely glued together and to the supporting rocks with a secretion from the salivary glands. Asiatic peoples have for centuries taken advantage of the nutritional value of bird saliva by boiling down the gelatinous nests of certain swiftlets (*Collocalia* spp.) to produce bird's-nest soup. The three to six eggs of the white-throated swift are white, spotted with excrement from the insects that infest the nests.

This species breeds from sea level to 13,000 feet in elevation from southern British Columbia and northwestern South Dakota to Honduras. It winters primarily from México south to Costa Rica, although a few remain as far north as central California, Arizona, New Mexico, and southern Texas.

PLATE 42

Anna's Hummingbird

CALYPTE ANNA

Bolting from his perch, the male streaked skyward until he was nearly lost from view above the treetops. Abruptly he turned and shot downward at a tremendous rate; and just before dashing himself against the limb where the object of his attention perched quietly and inconspicuously, he veered upward, producing an explosive *peek* sound. Continuing the arc, he reached a point directly above the same limb, where he suddenly hovered, body horizontal and bill down, and broke forth with his most tantalizing song—a long series of high-pitched gurgling squeaks. Thus the male Anna's hummingbird courts an intended mate.

In its breeding range, the Anna's hummingbird is confined to northern Baja California and that portion of California west of the Sierran divide. Preferring broad-leaved trees, especially along watercourses and in dooryards, this species has benefited greatly from the exotic flower plantings and permanent water supply provided by man. During the winter the Anna's hummingbird remains largely within its breeding range, although there are local movements, and some southern birds migrate eastward into southern Arizona and Sonora.

The two white eggs are deposited in a small cup-shaped nest that is constructed primarily of plant down strung together with spider webs and intricately embossed with lichens. The nest is placed from seventeen inches to thirty feet above the ground on virtually any type of support, including tree limbs, bushes, vines, and even power lines. At birth the bills of the young bear no resemblance to the lances carried by their parents, but instead are short and squat; full length is not attained until well after fledging. The feeding operation is enough to engender in the observer fear for the well-being of the nestlings. The adult female transfers her burden of insects and nectar by the process of regurgitation. To avoid wasting a morsel, she inserts her sword into the waiting mouth of a tiny offspring and rams it home to the hilt. She then pumps up and down with such violence that one must marvel that the youngster is not punctured or even pinned to the floor of the nest.

Most hummingbirds (family Trochilidae), including the Anna's, feed almost exclusively on nectar, spiders, and small insects, gleaning the latter from the local vegetation, spider webs, or even old sapsucker holes. Although their tiny mouths and slender bills would hardly seem to be adapted for fly-catching, hummingbirds spend much time at this pursuit, perching on an exposed site and darting quickly at any passing insect. Most feeding, however, is accomplished at flowers, especially those that are tubular in shape. Contrary to popular opinion, hummers are not more attracted by red than by other colors. The young birds apparently investigate any brightly colored object and learn by trial and error which present a suitable food source.

PLATE 42

ANNA'S HUMMINGBIRD, *Calypte anna*

Male (below) and female adults
Length: 3½-4 inches
Common monkey flower, *Mimulus guttatus*
Crotch's bumblebee, *Bombus crotchii* (queen)

PLATE 43

Rufous Hummingbird

SELASPHORUS RUFUS

Few birds are as territorial as hummingbirds, and few hummers are as territorial as the rufous. Staking out a feeding source, sometimes a feeding station, this pugnacious ball of animated lightning defends it against all comers. When a passing hummingbird enters the forbidden ground, the owner darts from his observation post and aggressively drives away the intruder. Occasionally, one chase may give rise to a chain reaction as the original combatants pass from one territory to another, until finally there results a general melee of flaming gorgets and flashing tails.

The courtship behavior of this species is similar to that of the Anna's hummingbird (*Calypte anna*). While a female perches demurely on the branch of a low bush, the male performs a towering ascent and dive. Reaching a point a few inches above her, he swoops upward and at the same time spreads his tail, which produces a whining sound as air rushes through the slender, stiffened outer feathers. In a more original performance, the male describes above the female a series of short, shallow arcs, accompanied by squeaking and tail-buzzing.

The hummingbird family (Trochilidae) is restricted to the New World. Of the some 320 species known, the rufous hummingbird occurs farthest to the north. It breeds from southeastern Alaska, southern Yukon, and western Montana south to northwestern California and southern Idaho. Because its annual fall migration begins so early—in the latter part of June—ornithologists once believed that this hummer bred in Colorado, New Mexico, and Arizona, but as yet no nest has been found in these states. During the winter months, unable to survive the cold climate prevalent in the northern coniferous forests in which it breeds, the rufous hummingbird migrates to México. Fall migrants move southward throughout the mountainous areas of the West, but are concentrated in the Rocky Mountains. In the spring the species follows a Pacific lowland route that provides more favorable weather conditions and hence a more abundant food supply (see Anna's hummingbird).

The nest of this species is much like that of Anna's hummingbird in structure, but is usually positioned within a few feet of the ground. The dimensions of the two (rarely one or three) white eggs average a petite 13.1 by 8.8 millimeters. The rufous hummingbird is somewhat colonial. As many as twenty nests, spaced a few yards apart, have been found within a small area. Favored nest sites may be reused from one year to the next, the second year's nest being positioned atop the eroded skeleton of the first, and the third year's nest on the combined hulk of the first and second.

RUFOUS HUMMINGBIRD, *Selasphorus rufus*

Male (above) and female adults
Length: 3¼-3¾ inches
Rattan's penstemon, *Penstemon rattanii*
West coast lady, *Cynthia annabella*

PLATE 44

Broad-Billed Hummingbird

CYNANTHUS LATIROSTRIS

Gathering its daily ration of energy-rich nectar, insects, and spiders, this feathered jewel dances from ocotillo to opuntia bloom. So small and active is the average hummingbird that it must ingest great quantities of food in order to sustain its high energy requirements. To avoid undue energy loss, it makes frequent rest stops, even clinging momentarily to a convenient perch while sipping a nectar cocktail.

Following the distribution of a number of species, the broad-billed hummingbird ranges from the southern portions of Arizona, New Mexico, and adjacent Texas south to southern México. Within this area, it seems to prefer riparian situations, where the parching effects of the torrid desert sun are minimized. The nest is placed usually within five feet of the ground and frequently along a stream bank or even directly over water. The plant downs, spider webs, and grasses that compose the bulk of the nest are adorned on the exterior with bits of dry leaves and bark, rather than the lichens that cover the nests of many hummingbird species. The broad-billed hummingbird shares several aspects of its breeding biology with virtually all other members of the hummingbird family (Trochilidae). The eggs are solid white and number two in a clutch. After mating, the polygamous male takes no part in nesting duties, but stands guard over his personal feeding territory, while his spouses build the nests, incubate the eggs, and feed the young.

The helicopter gyrations of a hummingbird are a wonder to behold. Hovering before a brilliant bloom, the bird suddenly hums backward, darts sideways to capture a passing insect, and finally flashes forward to stand on pumping tail in front of another flower. Unlike most birds, hummers are able to rotate their wings at the shoulder in such a manner that during the backstroke the underwing actually faces upward. Thus, the wing can deliver a supporting power stroke during both the up and down beats, producing the characteristic hovering action. The blurred-wing effect in flight is caused by the high rate of beating— over eighty beats per second in one species. As might be expected, the breast muscles, which provide the power for the wing strokes, are proportionately huge, in some species accounting for up to 30 percent of the total body weight. Relative to body size, the sternal keel of hummingbirds, which provides the base of attachment for these pectoral muscles, also attains its greatest development in hummingbirds.

PLATE 44

BROAD-BILLED HUMMINGBIRD, *Cynanthus latirostris*

Male (above) and female adults; female gathering nest material
Length: 3¼-4 inches

PLATE 45

Coppery-Tailed Trogon

TROGON ELEGANS

It may be argued, at least semantically, that the spectacular iridescent green feathers of the breast and upper body parts of a trogon are in reality black and that the green color as perceived by the human eye results merely from a trick of light. Unlike such colors as red, yellow, black, and brown, which are caused by the same chemical pigments as those found in flower petals, green usually is a structural color. In green trogon feathers, the barbules contain several layers of tubules composed of black pigment (melanin) enclosing air-filled spaces. When beams of light strike such a feather, some are reflected off the surface. Those that penetrate are refracted by the surface layer, then reflected by the underlying tubules, and finally bent again as they leave the feather. When the green wavelengths exit, they are in phase with those green rays originally reflected. Hence green color is reinforced and becomes visible to the eye. Other exiting colors are not in phase and are thus weakened or eliminated, resulting in the paradoxical situation in which light plus light equals darkness. When a trogon feather is so viewed as to change the angle of light incidence, different wavelengths emerge in phase to produce deep blue or golden hues. If one were to smash a green feather, the green-producing structure would be destroyed, revealing the pigment beneath and thus turning the feather black.

The coppery-tailed trogon occurs from southern Arizona and (casually) the lower Rio Grande valley of Texas south to Costa Rica. Our Arizona population, which retreats to northwestern México for the winter, occupies mixed forests of oak, ash, sycamore, walnut, and pine in semiarid canyons and mountain slopes from 6,000 to 8,600 feet in elevation. In southern México, the species also inhabits tropical deciduous forest at lower elevations. The Arizona birds are relatively fairly common and widespread in some years, but unaccountably rare during others.

For nesting, the coppery-tailed trogon utilizes abandoned woodpecker holes twelve to forty feet up in large trees, including oaks and sycamores. The cavity may be unlined or furnished with hay, straw, moss, vines, plant down, feathers, and other materials. The three to four (occasionally two) eggs are dull white to faintly bluish white.

In actions this species is slow and deliberate, and it tends to perch unobtrusively on a tree limb for long periods of time, its body nearly erect and tail hanging straight down. Occasionally, it darts out to snatch a flying insect or to hover momentarily while gleaning a fruit or larva from foliage. It is known to feed on wild grapes, cherries, grasshoppers, praying mantids, stinkbugs, and lepidopterous larvae. Its "song" is a loud hoarse *co-ah*, repeated six or seven times and said to resemble the call of a hen turkey (*Meleagris gallopavo*). When presenting this sound, the bird sharply elevates and then slowly lowers its tail.

Trogon is a Greek word meaning "gnawer," alluding to the serrated bill used to "gnaw" fruit. Because trogons apparently have no close relatives living today, they are placed in their own family, Trogonidae, and order, Trogoniformes.

PLATE 46

Green Kingfisher

CHLOROCERYLE AMERICANA

The green kingfisher is primarily a tropical and subtropical species. Widespread from México into South America, it is rare and local in the United States, reaching our borders only in southern Texas and south central Arizona. Its typical haunts are the shallow, often rock-studded streams and rivers where the water is crystal clear and the banks are wooded. In some localities it may frequent a quiet shallow pool or even venture into the brackish waters of a coastal lagoon. Perched motionless atop a midstream rock or snag or on an overhanging branch, it peers intently into the water. Intermittently, it emits a low click, accompanied by a perky twitch of the tail. Spotting a small minnow, it plunges headlong into the current and quickly returns with its prize. In flight this species is rapid and direct, and frequently all one sees is a green and white streak buzzing past low to the water and disappearing around a bend. Then from the distance one hears a sharp twittery rattle, as the bird voices its annoyance at being disturbed.

The kingfisher family, Alcedinidae, is cosmopolitan, absent only from certain islands and from the coldest regions. Of the 168 families of living birds, the Alcedinidae, with 87 species, ranks twenty-ninth in size. There are only three species in the Western Hemisphere north of the United States–Mexican border; and only one, the belted kingfisher (*Megaceryle alcyon*), is common and widespread. One characteristic shared by all members of the family is the strongly syndactyl feet. In the green kingfisher, for instance, the third and fourth toes are united for most of their length and share a single sole, while the second and third toes are joined basally. The majority of kingfisher species do not actually fish for a living, but use the same feeding techniques on land to acquire insects and small vertebrates. One aberrant type, the shovel-billed kingfisher (*Clytoceyx rex*) of New Guinea, digs in soil for earthworms, using its specially flattened bill as a shovel.

The female green kingfisher is similar to the male in appearance, but possesses a narrow strip of dark green spots in place of his chestnut breast band. The sexes share nesting duties. The nest is a cavity in a stream bank a few feet above the water. The entrance may be completely exposed or well hidden behind tree roots or overhanging leaves. The nest chamber itself is located at the end of a 2–3½-foot tunnel and is unlined. The three to six eggs are white, as are those of all kingfishers. Ants are perhaps the major predators on kingfishers. Entering a nest burrow, a voracious army pesters the incubating parent until, in shifting position, it accidentally breaks the eggs.

PLATE 46

GREEN KINGFISHER, *Chloroceryle americana*

Adult male
Length: 7-8½ inches
Bullhead minnow, *Pimephales vigilax*

PLATE 47

Acorn Woodpecker

MELANERPES FORMICIVORUS

The acorn woodpecker is aptly named, for it makes much of its living harvesting and storing vast quantities of acorns, which it retrieves at a later date when the vagaries of this seasonal food supply so demand. Choosing an appropriate site—the bark of a live oak or pine, a partially rotted tree limb or trunk, a telephone pole, or even the side of an old building—the woodpecker drills a hole of exactly the proper dimensions and then sallies forth to find an acorn. Returning to the hole, the bird inserts its prize small end first and pounds it flush. Since acorn woodpeckers are somewhat colonial, numerous birds share a storage site. Acorns may be placed in a density of two per square inch; and one such cache, an enormous pine, contained an estimated 50,000 acorns! Occasionally, carried away by its enthusiasm, a bird may store a cherry or date pit, or even a pebble.

Although much speculation has centered on the amount of damage caused by this instinctive behavior, studies have shown that the storage holes are usually harmless, rarely penetrating the living portions of the thick tree bark and piercing only the extreme outer layer of utility poles. As might be expected, these stores are a constant temptation to passing jays and squirrels and must be defended vigilantly by the ever-watchful picids. The would-be thief is attacked vociferously and with abandon, frequently by a band of woodpeckers, but nevertheless is successful often enough to warrant returning another day.

Acorns and other nuts, although comprising over 50 percent of the diet, are not the only food source. During the warmer months, the diet is varied with large quantities of insects, including ants, beetles, and flies, and with fruit such as cherries, apples, and figs. At times this rather ungainly woodpecker will flutter high into the air to obtain a passing insect on the wing. Sap is also a major item in the diet.

Whether defending its food or home, the acorn woodpecker is an amazingly energetic species. The parents share in the domestic duties—excavating the nesting cavity, incubating the four to six white eggs, and feeding the demanding young. Engaged in the last occupation, the industrious adults may return to the nest as often as twice per minute. While studying a nest, one observer saw a full-sized, but obviously immature woodpecker, probably the young from a previous nesting, aid the parents in the feeding of the nestlings. Such an assistant is termed a *helper*.

The raucous calls of the acorn woodpecker may be heard punctuating the stillness of oak forests from Oregon, western California, Arizona, and western Texas south to Panama. Like most members of its family (Picidae), this species is nonmigratory, choosing to spend the winter season ensconced atop its nutty storehouse.

PLATE 48

Lewis' Woodpecker

ASYNDESMUS LEWIS

"Typical" woodpecker behavior involves the scaling of tree trunks or limbs and the extraction of insects from holes that are drilled in wood. In order to occupy such a niche, ancestral woodpeckers evolved unique structural adaptations, including a straight, powerful bill and associated muscles for pounding, zygodactyl feet (two toes in front, and two behind), a stiffened tail for support in vertical clinging, and a long sticky tongue for catching insects in holes. With evolutionary proliferation of species, certain woodpeckers became secondarily adapted to other modes of existence, without, however, losing their basic picid anatomy. Such a bird is the Lewis' woodpecker. In feeding, this unusual species rarely uses its bill for boring or its tongue for the extraction of insects, nor does it spend much time in a vertical position on tree trunks. Instead, it engages in a variety of activities that belie its taxonomic relationships. About one-third of its food consists of acorns. Unlike the acorn woodpecker (*Melanerpes formicivorus*), which places its booty *in toto* in neatly fashioned holes, the Lewis' woodpecker breaks open the shells, extracts the meat, and stores it in natural crevices in trees or power poles. Each individual harvests, stores, and defends its own cache of nuts. Some birds forage extensively on the ground, where they obtain fallen acorns and various insects, including grasshoppers. During the fall, this species feeds to a large extent on fruit and may, on a local scale, become a pest in orchards. The most remarkable habit of the Lewis' woodpecker, however, is fly-catching. Scanning the sky from the top of an exposed snag, this bird suddenly sallies forth over a clearing, performs several circular maneuvers like a huge ungainly swallow, and returns with a flying ant, bee, or other insect. Apparently possessing remarkable eyesight, a bird of this species may fly over 100 feet to capture an insect seen from its perch. Significantly, the gape of the bill of *Asyndesmus* is unusually large for a woodpecker.

In direct flight, the Lewis' woodpecker exhibits none of the undulating motion common to its family (Picidae), but resembles a small crow, with strong steady strokes of its disproportionately broad wings.

This woodpecker was named in honor of its discoverer, Captain Meriwether Lewis of the famous Lewis and Clark Expedition of 1804–1806. During the breeding season it inhabits open pine or oak woodland, burns, forest edge, and riparian growth locally from southern British Columbia, western Alberta, Montana, and southwestern South Dakota south to southern California, central Arizona, and southern New Mexico and east to northwestern Nebraska and eastern Colorado. In winter this semigregarious species forms roving bands of up to 300 individuals, forsakes the more northerly portions of its range, and extends to such southern localities as western Texas, northern Sonora, and northern Baja California. It concentrates in oak woodlands, but also spreads into agricultural lands and even desert oases.

The single annual brood is raised by both parents in a hole that they excavate from four to 100 feet up in a living or dead tree. The four to nine (usually six or seven) eggs are white and moderately glossy. The nest cavity may be used for several successive years.

PLATE 49

Williamson's Sapsucker

SPHYRAPICUS THYROIDEUS

Probably no North American bird has had such a checkered nomenclatural history nor led avian taxonomists farther astray than the Williamson's sapsucker. The mystery began in 1851, when John Cassin, using a female specimen taken by J. G. Bell in Eldorado County, California, described a brown-and-black-barred woodpecker that he called *Picus thyroideus*. Three years later, in characterizing this "black-breasted woodpecker," Cassin stated that the sexes were similar in appearance, but that the female had less black on the chest and was somewhat paler throughout. In 1857, J. S. Newberry described as *Picus williamsonii* a striking "new" species, black, white, and yellow in color, which he had collected two years previously at Klamath Lake, Oregon, and had sexed as a female. Shortly thereafter (1860), Baird, Cassin, and Lawrence characterized the "male" of *williamsonii* as differing from the "female" type specimen only in the possession of a red rather than a white chin.

For fifteen years these strikingly different birds were treated as distinct species, and it was not until Henry W. Henshaw collected both a brown-barred female and a black, white, red, and yellow male as they left the same nesting cavity, that the mystery was solved: *thyroideus* and *williamsonii* were the same species! The brown-barred specimens of *thyroideus* thought to be males were in reality females, and the brightly colored type of *williamsonii* was a male, these specimens having been missexed. Furthermore, the supposed "female" of *thyroideus*, with its small black breast patch and pale color, is now known to be the immature female; and the white-throated "female" of *williamsonii* is the young male. Thus, the adult of each sex was considered the male of a species, and the immature of each sex was believed to be the female of a species. If the reader is now thoroughly confused, think how nineteenth century ornithologists must have felt, bewildered by missexed specimens and confronted by sexual plumage differences of a magnitude unique among North American woodpeckers.

The Williamson's sapsucker is widespread in western North America, breeding from western Montana and southern British Columbia south to northern New Mexico and southern California. During the summer it is confined to the higher portions of the mountains, where it inhabits forests of fir, spruce, and especially pine. Unlike most other members of its clan, the Williamson's sapsucker does not pound great chunks from its feeding tree, but rather fashions neat rows of small, evenly spaced holes, which then ooze sap to attract the sapsucker's insect food. Ants comprise a large portion of the diet, as do fibers from the cambium layer of evergreens.

All members of the woodpecker family (Picidae) nest in cavities, usually in trees, and lay unmarked white eggs. The Williamson's sapsucker is no exception, depositing its four to six white eggs in an unlined hole, which it excavates ten to fifty feet above the ground in a dead or dying tree.

WILLIAMSON'S SAPSUCKER, *Sphyrapicus thyroideus*

Male (above) and female adults
Length: 7½-8¾ inches
Quaking aspen, *Populus tremuloides*

PLATE 50

Ladder=Backed Woodpecker

DENDROCOPOS SCALARIS

The concept of adaptive radiation, the process of character divergence that enables related forms to exploit different opportunities in the environment, has long been recognized on the interspecific level, but has only recently been extended to the intrapopulation level. Under certain conditions, conspecific individuals may evolve polymorphism, often expressed in sexual dimorphism, that allows them to utilize different subdivisions of that niche occupied by the species as a whole. This polymorphism may be morphological, as in the case of the pygmy owl (*Glaucidium gnoma*), in which sexual disparity in size allows the exploitation of different prey; or it may be ecological, as with the ladder-backed woodpecker, which exhibits sexual separation in foraging sites. At one locality, for instance, male ladder-backed woodpeckers foraged exclusively on Joshua trees (*Yucca brevifolia*), spending 75 percent of their time on the trunks and branches and 25 percent on old seed clusters and new blossoms. Females, on the other hand, foraged 80 percent in cholla cacti and small bushes and only 20 percent in Joshua trees; of the latter amount, 17 percent was on new blossoms and only 3 percent on trunks and limbs. Such segregation allows the two sexes to coexist without undue competition.

Of the four species of woodpeckers (family Picidae) treated in this book, the ladder-backed is the most "typical" in its feeding habits. It probes, picks, pries, taps, and even, as a woodpecker should, excavates. Only occasionally does it deviate from this behavior by dropping to the ground. Over 90 percent of the food is animal matter, the bulk of which is composed of hemipterans, ants, and the larvae of beetles and lepidopterans. The vegetable portion of the diet includes the ripe figlike fruit of giant cacti.

This nonmigratory species inhabits heavily vegetated deserts and associated riparian growth up to 7,000 feet in elevation from the southern portions of California, Nevada, Utah, and Colorado south to Honduras and Nicaragua. Its westward spread in southern California seems to be limited in part by competition with the closely related Nuttall's woodpecker (*Dendrocopos nuttallii*), with which it sometimes hybridizes.

The nest is a cavity from two to thirty feet up in a dead or partially decayed branch of virtually any of the larger plant species in the habitat: cottonwood, oak, hackberry, willow, paloverde, mesquite, cardón cactus, agave, yucca, and various urban shade trees. The cavity is lined with wood chips that fall during excavation. The two to seven (usually three to five) eggs are pure white.

Although active and vociferous, this species adroitly escapes detection by keeping a limb or trunk between itself and the threat. The two commonest calls are a sharp *tschik*, apparently used both as a location call and a low-intensity alarm-threat, and a rattle, composed of a rapid series of the former notes. In conjunction with various displays, these birds produce several other vocalizations as well as a loud drumming, beaten at the incredible rate of about thirty taps per second.

LADDER-BACKED WOODPECKER, *Dendrocopos scalaris*

Male (right) and female adults
Length: 6-7½ inches
Mesquite, *Prosopis juliflora*

Index

Plates are indicated by *pl.* and primary species accounts by **boldface**.